Buck, Buck,
What's Up?

Buck, Buck, What's Up?

Tales from 60 Years in Journalism

TOM BUCK

Conversation Press, Inc.
WINNETKA, ILLINOIS

• • • • • • • • • • • • • • • •

This book is for my family. My wife, Ruth Luscombe Moss Buck. Our daughter, Mary-Moss Buck Young, and her husband, James Braham Young, M.D., and their daughter, Margaret Luce "Meg" Young. Our son, Thomas Luscombe Buck, and his wife, Deborah Stewart Buck, and their sons, Thomas Luscombe Buck, Jr., David William Buck and John Taylor Buck. My niece, Jane Buck.

The following articles, written by Tom Buck, are reprinted in this book with the permission of the Chicago Tribune Company, which owns the copyright for each story.

"Lil, A Waitress With a Big Heart," September 27, 1952
"CTA Collects a Lot More Than Fares," January 17, 1955
"Holiday Spirit Swamps Board," March 9, 1955
"Gifts and Feasts Told by Tribune Staffers," December 26, 1955
"Diary of Snake Bite Death," October 3, 1957
"Sheriff Pulls a Hat Trick," April 13, 1959
"The Littlest Dog Wags the Biggest Tale," September 27, 1971

The story of Chicago's father and son mayors, the Daleys and the Harrisons, originally printed in *LifeTimes*, published by Blue Cross and Blue Shield of Illinois, is reprinted with permission.

ISBN 0-9634395-9-6

Contents

From Indiana to Chicago

In the Service of Uncle Sam

My Years with the Tribune

●　●

There Is Life After Newspaper Reporting

●　●

Foreword

There was a time in Chicago when homing pigeons were used to transport news film and press rooms sported a bar.

And there was a time when veteran journalist Tom Buck had a ringside seat covering mayhem, monkey shines and major stories for 33 years from his desk at the *Chicago Tribune*.

For more than six decades, Buck has been doing what he loves best: viewing life from the back of a pen. Tom has decided, thank goodness, to take us for the reporter's ride of a lifetime in his book, *Buck, Buck, What's Up? Tales from 60 Years in Journalism*.

From the moment former President Truman, who had been excoriated editorially by Buck's paper, put his hand on Buck's shoulder and said, "You know, we all have had to play piano in a whorehouse at one time or another," we are taken on a journalistic tour of Chicago's news trenches.

From Buck's beginning as a Hoosier to his becoming a top reporter at one of the nation's largest newspapers, we are transported to Tom's view of the world from his perch.

I had the honor to watch Tom work when I started in the *Tribune's* newsroom in 1969. He was a star. And it's wonderful being able to watch his phosphorescence shine again in the pages of his book.

Michael Sneed, columnist
Chicago Sun-Times

Preface

This book is the result of many interesting hours spent during the noontime at the Members' Table of the Cliff Dwellers, the 96-year-old club quartered in a penthouse on Michigan Avenue across the street from the Art Institute of Chicago.

The Members' Table accommodates six to eight members who come to lunch alone and seek the company of others. Some days two Members' Tables are required to take care of everyone. Besides good conversation, there is complimentary red and white wine, which is provided by a generous member, Manly W. Mumford, who, as a bond lawyer, contributed a tax-exempt bond to cover the cost.

There is an unwritten rule against overly partisan political talk and making business deals at the table, but almost everything else can be the subject of the day. It is assumed that every story told is true—as true as anything can be in the face of the tricks memory can play.

For many years the Cliff Dwellers restricted its membership to men only, but at long last it was decided to catch up with the times by going co-educational. One of the delightful results has been that women can join in the storytelling at the Members' Table.

I would like to mention all the women and men storytellers I have enjoyed listening to, but I fear committing the gross error of leaving someone out. I do, however, want to mention three outstanding Cliff Dwellers who have passed on: Henry Regnery, Harry Malm and John McDermott.

Tom Buck, right, shares stories at the Cliff Dwellers Members' Table with, from left, Wilbert Hasbrouck and Leonard Foster.

Henry Regnery was a nationally known publisher who wrote a history of the Cliff Dwellers as one of his many literary contributions.

Harry Malm was our club librarian, a lawyer, college teacher and travel writer.

John McDermott was an unusual Chicagoan. He was an effective activist and observer in race relations, who, among his many activities, founded and edited *The Chicago Reporter*, a monthly civil rights publication sponsored by the Community Renewal Society.

Henry, Harry and John were regulars at the Members' Table for many years.

To my good fortune, it so happened that one of the Cliff Dwellers exposed to my storytelling at the Members' Table was Robert Bradner, a journalist who has moved into book publishing with his Conversation Press, Inc., based in Winnetka, Illinois. Bob has done me the honor of inviting me to put my stories on paper with the publication of this book. For this I will be forever grateful.

I wish to express my appreciation to Marilyn J. Hallett and her staff at her firm, Michigan Avenue Office Services, for transcribing this text from tape recordings.

More than anything else, I want to thank my wife, Ruth, for her advice and editing expertise, the worth of which is beyond calculation.

TOM BUCK

March 2003

From Indiana
to Chicago

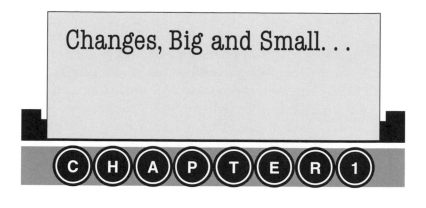

Changes, Big and Small. . .

To me, being a reporter is like being at the ringside of life—you are a neutral observer of people and whatever of interest may be going on. Also, I believe there should be a strong sense of creativity to search out the pertinent details and then arrange the information in a good storytelling format.

Best of all, I enjoy finding and telling stories about people that hit the human chord. I believe that an interesting story can be written about anyone and that the challenge often is finding it.

In my 60-plus years in journalism, it is unbelievable how much has happened in almost every field. The big things are obvious, but there are important little things that are likely to be overlooked.

As an example, homing pigeons played an unusual role in Chicago journalism before World War II. For the *Chicago Times*, a covey of homing pigeons served as full-time staff members.

The *Times* was a lively afternoon tabloid newspaper that featured photographs and good, terse writing. It later became a part of what is now the *Chicago Sun-Times*.

With the homing pigeons, the *Times* avoided street traffic jams in getting exposed film back to the newsroom. The pigeons were especially useful in meeting the afternoon deadline for the final edition that hit the streets shortly before 5 o'clock for commuters on their way home.

A *Times* photographer would go out on an assignment with a news camera in one hand and a small cage containing a pigeon in the other. The homing pigeons were ideal for covering baseball games in Wrigley Field on the North Side and Comiskey Park on the South Side.

For its late afternoon final, the *Times* often ran a front-page photo taken in the first inning of the baseball game. The photographer would make his shot, put the film in a capsule attached to the pigeon's leg and send the pigeon on its way downtown to the pigeon covey on top of the *Times'* building on Wacker Drive.

Here's another example of how things have changed.

In daily newspaper reporting, City Hall is without doubt the best beat in Chicago. Even if nothing is happening, it seems exciting; for something can happen at any minute without any notice.

During many years of my time working for the *Chicago Tribune*, I covered local government in Chicago and Cook County; and when the *Tribune's* regular City Hall reporter, Ed Schreiber, was on vacation, I filled in as a City Hall beat reporter.

It was the custom for Chicago's mayor to hold a daily press conference, if only to be available to answer questions the press might have. Once on a bright sunny day in July 1955 I was filling in for Ed on the City Hall beat. At that time, TV local news coverage had not been developed very fully, and there were only five reporters attending the daily press conference. These reporters were from the *Chicago Sun-Times,* the *Chicago Daily News,* the *Herald American,* the City News Bureau, a newspaper-owned news agency, and the *Chicago Tribune.*

The press room in the City Hall is on the second floor next to the City Council Chambers, and usually at around 10 A.M. the mayor's secretary, Miss O'Neil, would call from the fifth floor to say, "Okay, boys, he is ready to see you."

The mayor's press conference now is a big production, with radio and TV reporters, and at least four TV camera crews in attendance. Years ago, it was very informal. We reporters sat down in friendly fashion in front of the mayor in his office, although there could still be hardball questioning.

On that morning in July 1955, little or no news was expected as we sat down in front of the first Mayor Daley, Richard J. Daley, who had taken office only in April of that year. We were talking casually about the mayor's favorite baseball team, the White Sox, when all of a sudden former United States President Harry S Truman appeared in the doorway.

"Hi, Dick. I hope you don't mind my breaking in like this," President Truman said to Mayor Daley. "But I just wanted to drop by to say hello."

Truman had long been my favorite President, even though my paper, the *Tribune*, was very vicious about him in its editorials. The *Tribune* as much as said that Truman was so incompetent he couldn't find his way in and out of a telephone booth. But I knew him as a very competent and honest person, despite the smears published because early in his career he had been associated with the corrupt Pendergast political machine in Kansas City. Among other things, Truman was an accomplished pianist.

After giving Truman a warm greeting, Mayor Daley then began introducing us reporters to the former President.

When I was introduced as the *Tribune* reporter, Truman put his hand on my shoulder and said:

"You know your editors don't seem to think very much of me, and I really don't think very much of them. But I am sure you are an honorable young man, and you are just trying to make a good living, so you shouldn't worry too much about your employer. You know, we all have had to play piano in a whorehouse at one time or another."

After the laughter and the other introductions, we asked President Truman what had brought him to Chicago. Was there something special that he was doing here?

Truman said that he was attending some of the sessions of the Shriners' Convention, which was being held here; but he said his main reason for coming to Chicago was to collect items for his presidential library in Independence, his hometown near Kansas City.

As usual, he was staying at the Blackstone Hotel on South Michigan Avenue, and he said that early that morning he had walked up Michigan Avenue to the Tribune Tower. With his bodyguards unnoticed in the background, Truman liked to greet people while walking. Over the years many Chicagoans going to work were surprised to see a former President of the United States taking an early morning walk on Michigan Avenue.

That morning, Truman said, he had a special reason for visiting the Tribune Tower. At the entrance, he asked a guard where he could find Carey Orr, the *Tribune's* chief cartoonist. Not recognizing the former President, the guard said gruffly, "Just go over there and get on that elevator, and go up to the 23rd floor."

"I did as I was told," said Truman, "and when I got to the 23rd floor, I found that there was no receptionist there. So I walked around the corridor that went around the elevators in the center of the floor until I came to an office with a door partly open. At the top of the door was frosted glass with a name printed on it—Carey Orr.

"As I stepped in, Mr. Orr was at his easel drawing a cartoon. It probably was not very thoughtful of me, but I couldn't help peering over his shoulder to see what he was drawing.

"He apparently sensed that someone was looking over his shoulder, and he almost fell off his chair when he turned around and saw me.

"I apologized for dropping in on him like that, and then I told him that I was in Chicago to get things for my library in Independence. I asked him if he could give me a copy of the worst cartoon he had ever done on me.

"Mr. Orr still seemed a little bit shaken by my surprise visit, but he was very courteous and said that he was very honored and that he would give me at least a dozen or more."

Truman, who was a self-taught historian, told us that he considered cartoons to be very good historical records.

"If you can take a look at the best cartoons about a controversy, you can pretty well tell what the situation was all about," said Truman.

So it is that a collection of political cartoons is one of the special attractions at President Truman's presidential library in Independence.

It's very hard for me to believe such a story could unfold so casually today, which makes it a prized memory for me.

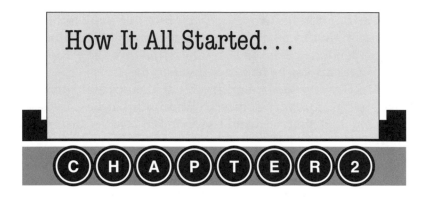

How It All Started. . .

C H A P T E R 2

To me, growing up in a small town in Indiana was the best of all worlds, even though many of those early years were during the Great Depression. While the Depression caused tremendous financial stress for many older people, as far as I can recall it made little or no difference for boys and girls in my hometown. Without money for expensive recreational equipment and activities, we had to be ingenious in making up things that were fun but didn't cost anything.

For organized sports and other activities, the school and churches were generally the centers of action. World War I veterans, as members of the American Legion, organized the Boy Scout troop, and sponsored other community activities such as the observance of Memorial Day, the staging of carnivals and circuses, and the celebration of the 4th of July.

There was sandlot baseball in the summer, fall and spring. And, as the world knows, it wouldn't have been Indiana without basketball. Every town, regardless of its size, had basketball in the junior high and high school. March was the wild month, with the sectional, regional and state basketball tournaments being played.

Then there was music. The piano was played only by girls because boys thought that was too sissy. But many of us enjoyed playing instruments in the band and orchestra at school, and at special events and band concerts in the summer.

We had a wonderful bandmaster, Charles Byfield, who taught at four schools, and who put his pupils at the various schools together in a band numbering more than 100 players. Regardless of the Depression, the means were found to send our combined band to various out-of-town special events. Our most noteworthy trip was in 1934 when we played at Indiana Day at the Chicago World's Fair.

For our World's Fair concert, we shared the stage with Indiana Governor Paul McNutt; George Ade, a Hoosier playwright and author; and John T. McCutcheon, the noted *Chicago Tribune* cartoonist.

I went along as a clarinetist who couldn't play because I had broken a finger playing baseball. I was thrilled to be master of ceremonies for our World's Fair appearances.

Besides Star City, the three other schools with players in our combined band were in Monterey, Pulaski and Royal Center.

Let me backtrack a little to explain that I was born on March 18, 1917, in a small Indiana town that was first named Scarborough but then was changed for easier spelling to Star City. With a population of 500, Star City is in Pulaski County in the north central part of Indiana, about 100 miles from Chicago.

It is a farming area, where my great-great-grandfather, Thomas Buck, settled in the early 1830s after he and his wife, Elizabeth Blue Buck, had moved with their 11 children from the southwestern tip of Ohio near Cincinnati. They must have had two covered wagons to make the trip.

As a Hoosier pioneer, my great-great-grandfather became very active in the community. He was the officially appointed fence-watcher to settle disputes over newly surveyed farm boundaries. He was active with the Horse Protective Association and also handled public welfare cases.

He donated an acre of his farm for use as one of the first public cemeteries in Pulaski County. The Buck Cemetery, which is still well-tended, is near the small town of Thornhope, about three miles south of Star City.

My mother, whose maiden name was Maud Kauffman, was a schoolteacher who persisted in getting a higher education, although that was not common in those years. The first place my mother taught was a one-room schoolhouse about two miles from her home. She lived with her father and two sisters in Harrison Township north of Star City. My grandfather, John Kauffman, who was a farmer, went to the schoolhouse early every winter morning to start the fire in a space heater so that the school would be warm when Mother and the pupils arrived.

Grandfather Kauffman was a very determined person— you might say, downright stubborn. He thought that the one-room schoolhouse was not good enough and that a better building should be provided. The township trustee, who was the school administrator, did not agree and insisted that the old one-room school building was all that was needed.

One cold morning, my mother and the pupils arrived at school to find it had burned to the ground. There was a rumor that instead of starting a fire in the stove, my grandfather had set the building on fire that morning; but no one was able to prove it, and my grandfather made no comment.

My father, Grover Buck, was a telegrapher on the Panhandle Branch of the Pennsylvania Railroad. He worked in the railroad tower at the south edge of Star City and was credited with having saved the life of a woman trying to commit suicide when he grabbed her and pulled her off the tracks as a fast train was approaching.

He died from the flu on March 4, 1920, when he was only 36 years old and had been ill for less than a week. Everyone in our family had been hit by the flu except for my brother, Ralph, and me. He was one year old, and my third birthday was coming up in two weeks.

The night before my father died, our house caught on fire. He was taken to the home of our next-door neighbors, Dr. and Mrs. Edward Johnston. Most of the second story of our house was destroyed.

Fortunately, Frank Marker, the township trustee, who was the school administrator, was looking for a teacher to fill a vacancy for the fifth and sixth grades at the Star City school. It was decided that Mother could step in on a temporary basis, pending taking more courses to bring her license up to date. For that first summer, while Mother was at the Terre Haute Teachers College, I stayed with my father's sister, Aunt Josie, and her husband, Everett Day, who lived on a farm near our town.

I spent two summers with them while Mother was at the teachers' college in Terre Haute. I remember those summers as very delightful times.

Growing up in a small town like Star City offered many activities. We liked to wander along Mud Creek and catch catfish and sunfish. Mud Creek, which was a very old ditch just south of town, was only a foot or so deep at the most, but we still liked to get in the water, either to wade or just sit.

On a hot day, we would strip down to our birthday suits near a railroad bridge and as a passenger train rolled by, we would jump up and down waving our arms. The railroad passengers must have thought we were either crazy or simply rural delinquents.

Sadly, Mud Creek and other streams in that area, including the picturesque Tippecanoe River, are now so polluted that no one can either swim or fish in them.

It may have been the Great Depression, but there were many ways to earn money, even in a small town. Mowing a lawn paid 15 to 25 cents. The going rate for working on a farm or doing other manual labor was a dollar a day, for 10 hours at 10 cents an hour. For a day at farm work, there always was a free lunch, usually fried chicken.

I once had a good early morning job as janitor of the Star City Bank, thanks to a great-uncle, Fielden Buck, the bank president. For a six-day week, I was paid 50 cents a morning for a total of $3 for the week.

With part of the janitorial earnings, I opened my first savings account in the bank and had saved a total of $35 when Franklin D. Roosevelt became President in 1933. As old-timers will remember, one of the first things President Roosevelt did was to have all the banks closed to straighten out the nation's financial situation. Only the banks that were found to be sound were allowed to reopen.

Unfortunately, our Star City bank did not reopen, and depositors were paid 10 cents on the dollar for their savings. I received for my $35 in savings a refund of $3.50, although I considered the hardest blow to be that of having lost the janitorial work.

For me, however, the best job of all was one that ultimately helped lead me to become a journalist; and that's the next story.

As far back as I can remember, I had always wanted to be a journalist. I was interested in both newspapers and radio newscasts.

My hero was Lowell Thomas, the network newscaster who had started out years before as a Chicago newspaperman. I never missed his nightly newscast with his sign-off, "So long until tomorrow." I distinctly remember his broadcast in 1933 when Hitler came to power.

As I look back, I realize that I really first got the bug to become a journalist when I started as a newspaper carrier. That began in fifth grade (age 11) and continued through high school. The preceding carrier, Jeanette Fry, a neighbor of ours, had recommended me for the job when she graduated from high school. From then on I had printer's ink in my blood, as the saying goes.

The paper, *The Pharos-Tribune*, was published 20 miles away in Logansport, and my bundle of papers was dropped from a bus about 4:30 every afternoon at Groom's Drugstore.

My brother, Ralph, often helped me by handling a part of the route that stretched out along a road in what we called "String Town." At the most, I had 90 subscribers — almost every home in town plus most of the stores. Subscribers paid me 10 cents for a six-day week of papers. The papers cost me 6 cents, so 4 cents was my profit. Not only was I making good money, though, but perhaps more important, I was in the newspaper business.

There's an old saying in journalism that a habit of reading is necessary to be a good journalist and that it really makes no difference what you read, just as long as you read. Besides reading the afternoon *Pharos-Tribune*, which I carried, I also read the *Logansport Press*, a morning newspaper, and on Sundays we bought either the *Chicago Tribune* or the *Indianapolis Star*, or both. (The Sunday *Tribune* cost 10 cents at the time.)

In addition to newspapers, I read the weekly *Saturday Evening Post* from cover to cover, along with other publications such as the monthly *American* magazine and *Boy's Life*, published by the Boy Scouts of America. Another of my favorite publications was *The Classmate*, which our Methodist church distributed free every Sunday.

I especially enjoyed reading history, biographies and historical novels. I read one book five times—*The Crisis*, a Civil War novel by Winston Churchill (the American author, not the British prime minister). Another favorite was *A Man Without a Country* by Edward Everett Hale.

There was no public library in our town, but we could get books by writing the Indiana State Library in Indianapolis.

We didn't have a typewriter, so I put together my own make-believe newspapers by hand-lettering the stories and putting them together in the form of a newspaper page layout on large pieces of white paper.

As a senior in high school, I founded our first school newspaper, a monthly which I named the *Star Review*. A transfer student, Bill Coulson, was the only one in our school who could type, so he helped me put out the paper, which we then mimeographed. To me it was a creative challenge that was a lot of fun.

As a newspaper carrier, I also had an opportunity to gain experience as a salesman. As part of circulation campaigns, the management of the *Pharos-Tribune* sent their carriers to other towns to solicit subscribers by going door to door to explain the benefits of getting the *Pharos-Tribune* every day.

One year I signed up enough new subscribers in other towns to win a three-day visit to Chicago, where, as a group of a dozen winning carriers, we stayed at a major downtown hotel, visited museums and saw a big league baseball game. The only mishap was that we made ourselves sick by eating too much at a Thompson cafeteria, for which Chicago was famous.

After all the reading, the years spent delivering newspapers and my early journalism efforts at school, I definitely decided in my freshman year at Indiana University to become a newspaper reporter and writer. That decision came about as if it were meant to be.

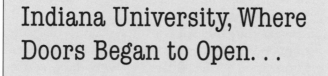

Indiana University, Where Doors Began to Open. . .

CHAPTER 3

I decided to go to Indiana University in Bloomington at the last minute, just one month before the fall semester began in 1935. It turned out to be one of the best decisions I ever made.

Originally, I had hoped to go to DePauw University, the Methodist-sponsored university in Greencastle, Indiana. I had placed a $5 deposit for a room in a dormitory after getting an indication that I would get a good scholarship. About the first of August, however, I was informed by DePauw that there had been a great demand for scholarships and that my request had to be turned down.

I was, however, able to get one of two I.U. scholarships that were available for our county. The I.U. scholarship covered the tuition, which amounted to $75 for the year. That sounds unbelievable now, but $75 was a lot of money in the Depression.

While discussing my plan to go to I.U., my bandmaster, Charles Byfield, told me that his brother, George, was leaving Bloomington after having completed his pre-med work to go to the I.U. Medical School in Indianapolis and that his room in a Bloomington private home probably was still available. I followed up immediately and was able not only to reserve the room at only $2 a week but also to gain a roommate who was a junior in journalism and an editor of the I.U. student newspaper.

As it turned out, this was not just a good place to stay, but it also opened the gate to my future in newspaper work.

My roommate, J.E. O'Brien, who has retired to Bloomington after a career in journalism, has been a wonderful life-long friend.

Through J.E., I immediately became well acquainted with the journalism students and their work in putting out the I.U. newspaper, the *Daily Student*.

It was an introduction to journalism that would have been impossible for a freshman to obtain otherwise. Freshmen were not supposed to work on the *Daily Student*, but I was able to write small stories on my own because of my acquaintance with J.E. and the staff.

I felt that our *Daily Student* group, which was co-educational, was truly unique. For me, the paper route, my reading habit and the fascination with news had all come together, and I was certain that journalism would be my career.

The *Daily Student* covered national and international news, and university life, which included everything from Big Ten sports to performances by nationally known dance bands of the "Big Band" era. During my years at I.U. (1935-1939), we had the Associated Press wire service to strengthen our coverage. That was particularly important because those were the years of increasingly aggressive acts by Hitler in the prelude to World War II.

At the *Daily Student*, when we received an AP story about a major move by Hitler and the Germans, one of us would interview a political science professor for a news analysis story to run as a sidebar to the AP story.

We also kept up with national and international affairs by inviting professors to address weekly luncheons sponsored by our I.U. chapter of Sigma Delta Chi, a professional journalistic fraternity. As Sigma Delta Chi members, we were fortunate in having our own private lounge in the Union Building for lunches and other activities.

Our studies also supported these interests, as it was common to combine a journalism major with a political science minor. This included classes on the various levels of American government, an introduction to international law and a course on foreign governments.

We took turns writing news-analysis types of columns. In one instance, I learned how easy it can be to hurt someone's feelings without having any intention of doing so. I wrote a column lamenting the fact that independent grocers were beginning to be forced out of business by competition from chain stores (now supermarkets). I don't know how my column came to his attention, but an independent grocer in my hometown, Sam Simmermaker, told me that he had been insulted because he felt I was writing about him and his store.

All of this was good training, but it also took good mentors. During my time at I.U., we had two journalism professors who had a paternal approach to their teaching.

Our foremost mentor was J. Wymond French, who also was the faculty advisor for the *Daily Student*. For journalism students, the 1930s at I.U. are remembered as the J. Wymond French years.

To all of us on the *Daily Student*, he was a surrogate father. He was gentle but firm in his criticism. He was on hand every night to inspect all copy, but he never told anyone what to write except to correct major errors. He did explain how we might improve the writing of a news or feature story. The next day the pages of the *Daily Student* would be on a bulletin board with Professor French's notations and corrections in red ink.

Professor French taught the important course on reporting and writing, but his most fascinating course was in foreign reporting. He depicted the John Gunthers of the day as super-celebrities and true role models.

The other helpful professor was Joseph A. Wright, who was faculty advisor for the summer issues of the *Daily*

Student and for a special newspaper published by I.U. students during the late August State Fair in Indianapolis.

I worked on the State Fair newspaper staff for two years. There were eight of us who stayed on the fairgrounds and sent our copy every evening by a special carrier to Bloomington, where the papers were printed and then brought to Indianapolis early the next morning.

Professor Wright scanned our copy with an approving eye and usually gave no advice unless we asked for it.

At the start of the first day, however, he took us boys aside for a short lecture. He warned us about a red light district in Indianapolis (which we had never heard about) and said that horrible things could happen to us if we chanced to go there. Everyone took his advice—that is, as far as I know.

In my senior year, Professor Wright gave me an opportunity to earn a little money by helping him critique high school newspapers. He headed a special program of giving constructive criticism to high schools submitting their newspapers and other publications for review.

I made straight A's in the journalism courses, and A's and B's in political science. My lack of interest in other courses was reflected by "gentleman C's."

For most of my four years at Indiana University, working on the *Daily Student* seemed to be the only thing that counted, even in one's sleep.

I realized that fact of I.U. life one Saturday night in a maternity hospital in Indianapolis.

A friend and I had hitchhiked from Bloomington to enjoy a Saturday evening at a popular collegiate tavern on the Circle in downtown Indianapolis. We had a friend who was an intern at the Coleman Maternity Hospital where, he said, there were always extra beds in the interns' dormitory. We could slip in a back door and take an elevator to the dormitory unnoticed.

It was about midnight when we got to the dormitory and found that we were the only ones there. So, we picked out spare beds and went to sleep.

I don't know how long the telephone had been ringing, but I finally stumbled to a phone on the wall, grabbed the receiver and said, *"Daily Student."*

An anxious voice, apparently of a nurse, shot back, "I don't care what kind of a student you are. Get down here at once! We have one on the way, and we need help."

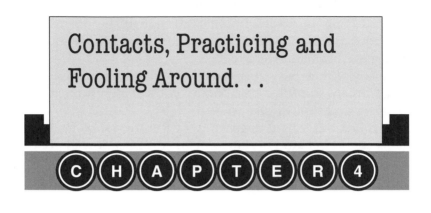

Contacts, Practicing and Fooling Around. . .

C H A P T E R 4

One of my early stories for the I.U. newspaper, the *Daily Student*, resulted in an unexpected aftermath nine years later.

As a sophomore in the fall of 1936, taking the required course in the Reserve Officer Training Corps (ROTC), I discovered that the *Daily Student* did not cover the military department. So, I began turning in bits of ROTC news on my own.

One story was about the men's rifle team winning the Big 10 championship. The team was coached by Major T.F. Wessels.

When the story ran, I got a call to see Major Wessels in his office right away. My first thought was that I must have done something wrong, for Wessels had a reputation of being a stern officer. As I entered his office, Wessels exclaimed, "That was a great story you wrote!

"I don't know how you got it in the paper, because the *Daily Student* editors have never really printed anything about us before. We have felt the paper never liked us."

For me, that was the start of an unusual friendship.

The next week, when our ROTC platoon was "falling in" for a drill session, Major Wessels came up and said, "Private Buck, you are now a corporal. Get your chevrons sewed on."

Although I appreciated the promotion, I had not yet taken the time to get the chevrons sewed on when two weeks later, Major Wessels came up again. "Corporal Buck, get those chevrons on because I would hate to have to demote you."

That time, as Corporal Buck, I did as I was told.

After my sophomore year, and the end of my ROTC, however, I had no occasion to see Major Wessels again. That is, not until the fall of 1945. I was a first lieutenant at the SHAEF (Eisenhower) headquarters in Frankfurt, Germany, on routine duty while awaiting orders to go home.

Behind the headquarters building was a two-story casino. The junior officers ate on the first floor, and the generals and other senior officers on the second floor.

One noon as I was going through the crowded casino lobby, a loud voice sounded: "Buck! You old son of a gun, how are you?"

I was so surprised that it took me a minute or two to find my voice.

"Major Wessels, how are you?" I blurted.

A nearby colonel admonished me. "Lieutenant, you are talking to a general!"

"Colonel, this young man can call me anything he wants to," said General Wessels. "He's an old friend of mine from Indiana University." Then it dawned on me that Wessels was wearing the star of a brigadier general.

A week later General Wessels invited me to lunch, during which he made me an offer to join him for the next year as an aide with the rank of captain. He had just received a very interesting assignment. He was to work in Zurich, Switzerland, flying in and out of Russia and other parts of Europe as a top administrator of a major program for returning thousands of displaced people to their homelands.

He gave me a week to think it over, and he was very understanding when I turned him down. Despite his generosity, after almost five years, I felt I had had enough of Army life.

In the latter part of my junior year at I.U., an unusual incident occurred that could have made radio journalism my career.

The Pontiac Division of General Motors was sponsoring weekly NBC radio broadcasts of variety shows from university campuses. The one-hour variety shows featured campus bands and talented student performers. Students also were used as the main announcers to give the commercials. The shows represented good public relations for the universities.

It was Indiana University's good fortune to be selected for one of the shows. About three weeks before the broadcast, an NBC producer, Paul Dumont, arrived on campus to make preparations. As a *Daily Student* reporter, I interviewed him every day for a story about his plans.

A popular student dance band led by Jimmy Cathcart was a natural selection for the show. To choose individual students, Dumont depended mostly upon the School of Music and the Speech Department for recommendations.

As a journalist, I was not in the running for a place on the show, although I was blessed with a good, deep voice. Two days before the broadcast, however, Dumont told me that he still needed a main announcer with a strong voice, and he asked if I would like to be it.

As it turned out, it sounded as if I were a regular NBC announcer giving the opening and closing announcements, as well as the commercials.

On the day of the show, I telephoned an uncle, George Warne, in Chicago to tell him to listen in because of his interest in radio productions. As an advertising executive, Uncle George was closely involved in the weekly production of the "National Barn Dance." After hearing me on the Pontiac Varsity show, Uncle George called me to suggest that I come to Chicago for a tryout as an announcer with WLS, a major station, which at that time was owned by *The Prairie Farmer,* a popular farm publication.

I lost no time in getting to WLS in Chicago, and I did very well with the announcing test, which for the most part involved reading copy that one was seeing for the first time.

However, there was more to the tryout. I was asked two questions:

"Do you play a guitar and can you sing country music?"

I could do neither, and it was explained to me that WLS could only afford to hire announcers who also could sing and play a guitar.

At the *Daily Student* each year there were four editors-in-chief, giving as many students as possible an opportunity to serve in that position. An editor-in-chief was given a free hand to do what he or she pleased without any interference whatsoever by a faculty advisor.

Professor Alfred Kinsey, who was to become famous as a pioneering sex researcher, gave us at the *Daily Student* an opportunity to spice up the paper with unusual articles.

He was propelled into the limelight as a sex expert in Bloomington when it was announced that he would give a lecture on sex as part of a new course on marriage. Until then, Kinsey had been known as an expert on gall wasps.

The marriage course had been added to the curriculum at the suggestion of a group of serious-minded coeds who were interested in broadening the university's approach to life. The course, which was an elective, was quickly over-subscribed, largely because of the interest in Kinsey's sex lecture.

For the benefit of students in general, we at the *Daily Student* covered this and subsequent sex lectures by Kinsey, being careful to use only language appropriate for a family newspaper.

During my last year at Indiana University some people in my hometown of Star City believed that I had gotten into trouble by producing an obscene show on the campus. They got this idea from reading a short article in an Indianapolis newspaper which had a picture of me and another student behind bars in the city jail in Bloomington. It was a confusing story and picture about an unusual event.

Each spring our chapter of Sigma Delta Chi sponsored a Gridiron Banquet patterned somewhat after the Gridiron Banquet held in Washington, D.C. Our Gridiron Banquet was held in Alumni Hall of the Union Building, and it attracted more than 400 students and faculty members.

In a series of skits, we razzed well-known students and faculty members, using rumor and gossip more than facts and truth. As a matter of fair play, we called upon a faculty member to give a return razz, taking us Sigma Delta Chi members apart as we did the students and faculty.

For the Gridiron Banquet in my senior year we had invited Professor Fowler Harper, a prominent member of the law school faculty, to give the return razz.

Professor Harper was on the stage and had just begun his presentation when all of a sudden six Indiana state policemen came bursting into the hall.

Leading the police detail as their chief was Don Lash, a former I.U. track star.

Taking over the microphone on the stage, Lash announced:

"Please keep your seats and don't get excited. We are here to arrest two students on a charge that they have been the ringleaders in putting on a lewd and obscene show on the I.U. campus.

"These two students will be taken immediately to the City Jail downtown, and there will be a trial in about an hour at the courthouse."

Paul Boxell, who had written most of the show, and I, as president of our Sigma Delta Chi chapter, were arrested; but we sensed that this was a stunt arranged by Professor

Tom Buck (left) and Paul Boxell were photographed in the Bloomington, Indiana, city jail during Tom's final year of college, to the great distress of some people in his hometown.

Harper. Many of the students and faculty members in the audience apparently thought it was authentic, and a number of them went downtown for the court session.

The special session of court was convened by Mayor Loba (Jack) Bruner of Bloomington, although because of several interruptions the trial never got underway.

Apparently believing this was a real case, the I.U. comptroller, Ward G. Biddle, asked Mayor Bruner if he could post bail for us so that the trial could be held under calmer conditions.

The prosecuting attorney was drawn into a heated verbal exchange with Professor Alfred Kinsey, who apparently was coming to our defense. At that point the mayor called the whole thing off, explaining that the arrests had been arranged by Professor Harper as a return razz for our Gridiron Banquet.

The people in my hometown would never have known about any of this had it not been for Paul Boxell's brother, Vern, who was news editor of the *Indianapolis Times*. He had come to our Gridiron Banquet to see what Paul had written for the show, and before driving back to Indianapolis, he arranged for a photographer to take a picture of Paul and me behind bars in the jail. That picture, along with a short story, appeared in the *Indianapolis Times* a day or so later.

The story gave the impression that this was a true case, so you could hardly blame my hometown folks for getting the wrong idea when they saw the picture and the story.

On to Chicago and the City News Bureau. . .

CHAPTER 5

The City News Bureau was founded in 1899 to provide coverage of basic news sources and to train new reporters for Chicago's daily newspapers. The Bureau was owned by the Chicago newspapers and ceased operations in 1999, 100 years later, because the base of financial support had narrowed so much that the surviving dailies, the *Chicago Tribune* and the *Chicago Sun-Times,* no longer felt that City News was the most economical way of obtaining these basic services.

In my time and for years before and after, the chance to work at the City News Bureau was one of the best things that could happen to a beginning journalist. It was the very best place in the world to learn to be a good and accurate reporter. The experience of digging up facts and particularly of checking facts was invaluable. It also provided a great opportunity to develop the skills of asking questions, another necessary attribute for being a good reporter.

But it was almost overwhelming. There was so much to do and so little time to do it. A City News reporter could not relax a minute if he or she were doing the job correctly, even to take time out for a decent lunch.

There were no fixed deadlines because every minute was a deadline. The objective was to get police, court and local government stories as quickly as possible to the newspapers which jointly owned the Bureau. Most of the information from reporters was phoned in to rewrite men; seldom, if ever, did a reporter get to write a story.

Until television news coverage began to develop in the 1950s, newspapers held a virtual monopoly on news. There was radio news, but it was relatively insignificant as daily competition compared to the intense competition among newspapers. Multiple editions, each with its deadline, were the rule. This required the City News Bureau to provide a flow of information as fast as possible.

The afternoon newspapers put out editions between 9 A.M. and 5 P.M., while the morning papers started editions at 5 P.M. and could still be "replating" editions as late as 6 A.M.

In the field of real estate, brokers say that the paramount value is "location, location, location." At City News, it was "accuracy, accuracy, accuracy." Making an error concerning a name or address was a cardinal sin. I knew one beginner who was fired on the afternoon of his first day because of several errors with names. It was a time in Chicago when veteran politicians would say, "I don't care what you write about me, but be sure to spell my name and title right."

I owe my start in Chicago to the timely help of two men—E. Ross Bartley and Isaac Gershman. Bartley gave me an all-important letter of introduction, and Gershman hired me as a cub reporter.

Several years before my graduation in 1939, Ross Bartley had come to Indiana University as public relations director and head of the I.U. News Bureau after having had an outstanding career in Chicago and Washington, D.C. As an Associated Press reporter, he covered the White House during the presidency of Warren G. Harding and then served as press secretary to Vice President Charles Dawes.

When his service as Vice President was over, Dawes returned to Chicago and brought Bartley with him to handle public relations for the banking operations of the

Dawes family. Bartley's association with the Dawes family enabled him to become the director of public relations for the Chicago Century of Progress World's Fair in 1933 and 1934.

Jobs were hard to get because of the Depression, and I was very fortunate three months before graduation to have had a job promised to me by the managing editor of the *Indianapolis Times*. Notwithstanding this, Bartley said he might be able to help me get a job in Chicago if I were interested.

Bartley's letter of introduction for me was to Gershman, who was managing director of the City News Bureau. About six weeks before graduation Bartley suggested I go to Chicago with the letter of introduction to see Gershman. I made the trip the very next weekend, but I was unable to see Gershman because he was in a hospital recovering from an automobile accident. I left the letter with his secretary.

Only about two weeks before graduation I learned from a friend in Chicago that I probably would get a City News Bureau job if I went back for an interview with Gershman.

I wasted no time in getting there, and I became one of four new reporters hired that June. Among other things, Gershman, who was from Lowell, Indiana, said he took special pleasure in hiring me because I was the first Hoosier he had an opportunity to hire at City News in a number of years.

The three others hired at that time were John T. McCutcheon, Jr., son of the *Tribune* cartoonist, who would become chief editorial writer for the *Tribune*; Kermit Holt, who became travel editor of the *Tribune*; and Gail Compton, who became farm editor of the *Tribune* and then pioneered in television with a popular program about pets.

We were really hired only as temporary employees for the summer to help cover during the vacation season. The understanding was that we would continue at City News in the fall if vacancies had developed in the meantime.

The salary of a beginning City News reporter was $20 a week, and there was an additional $5 for streetcar fare. The fare at that time was only 7 cents. A ride in a taxicab was permitted only in an emergency and could be taken only by authorization by the city editor at City News.

A City News reporter became well acquainted with local government, but by far the hardest work of all was a daytime beat covering the police or the courts. For police reporting, City News had an experienced reporter at the Central Police Station and then divided the city into three police reporting beats. Such a beat would cover at least a dozen police stations, as well as other sources of news, such as police courts and the holding of inquests by the coroner's office.

On weekdays a daytime police reporter had to check out at least a half-dozen coroner cases by contacting the deputy coroner or a policeman who may have been present at an inquest. The inquests concerned unnatural deaths, and most were held in funeral homes.

As a routine procedure, the police reporter had to check each of his dozen or so stations by police telephone each hour. Most of the police desk sergeants were very helpful, although a few could be very nasty and of little or no help.

During an eight-hour shift, a day police reporter also was supposed to visit at least four or five of the major stations in search of news and to get acquainted with the policemen, particularly the detectives.

An enterprising reporter could pick up some very good short feature stories by checking the police courts. Most judges of these courts were very helpful in identifying stories and notifying reporters of cases they might otherwise miss.

On the daytime police beats, however, the problem of checking the routine matters was so time-consuming that there was often little or no opportunity to develop news stories.

My third day at the City News Bureau was without doubt one of the most hectic experiences I have ever had. After riding streetcars all day to cover police stations, reporters had to return to the City News office in the Loop to check out. A reporter even had to account in detail for all assignments that were not worth stories.

At the end of that third day, I returned to the office almost in a state of panic. We had been hired on the condition that we could be fired at anytime if we didn't do the job right.

There was one assignment I had no information on at all. It was the death of a 95-year-old lady who had lived on the far Southeast Side of Chicago, almost in Indiana.

She had been listed as a coroner's case simply because there had been no doctor to sign the death certificate. The coffin and the body were at her home, and the funeral director had no information worth anything. The police knew nothing, and the coroner's office could not have cared less.

The editor at the City News Bureau office said I had a choice: I could either forget about it and get fired or go to the home.

It was a long streetcar ride, involving two transfers, and it was almost 9 o'clock when I got there. I had a feeling that I was the only one who had come to the wake. Maybe neighbors and friends had been there earlier.

The only person there was a bachelor brother with whom the woman, a spinster, had lived. He seemed glad to see me and invited me to sit down with him in front of the coffin.

I was bound and determined by then to get a story. Remember, this lady was 95 and it was 1939, so much of her life had been before the turn of the century.

I kept asking where she had worked, and finally he mentioned something about Prairie Avenue. That rang a bell historically. In the 1890s, Prairie Avenue, on the near South Side, was prominent as the neighborhood of mansions of Chicago's richest people.

"Did your sister do housework on Prairie Avenue?" I asked.

"Oh, no," he said. "Nothing like that. She was a very good dressmaker, a seamstress, and she made dresses for women like Mrs. Marshall Field, Mrs. Potter Palmer, Mrs. Philip Armour, Mrs. Swift and others like that."

"You're sure of this?" I asked.

Sensing my disbelief, he left the room for a few minutes and then came back with some old yellowed newspaper clippings.

The clippings verified the story, telling how his sister had once been known as the favorite seamstress of Prairie Avenue.

From my City News story, all the Chicago papers the next day carried long stories about the seamstress of Prairie Avenue, whose death almost went unnoticed.

One morning, on the West Side police beat, I took the risk of letting everything else go to follow up on what appeared to be an intriguing story.

As the first stop on the beat, I was in a station just off "Skid Row," an area in which homeless men lived in cheap hotels. Many of the men on Skid Row were alcoholics, but not all of them. Some were simply older men who had no families and were forced to live in inexpensive housing because of low incomes.

As I entered the police station, an older man was shouting at the top of his voice.

"I'm alive!" he cried. "I'm alive, I'm alive, I'm alive! But no one will be believe me!"

The desk sergeant had apparently had enough.

"Get out of here and don't come back!" he yelled, reinforcing his command by throwing a Chicago telephone book at the old man.

Ducking the telephone book, the man continued shouting, "I'm alive! I'm alive! I'm alive!" as he went out.

I followed him out and quickly caught up with him.

"Take it easy," I said, "and tell me what is bothering you."

It took him a few minutes to calm down before he could tell me his story.

His name was Richard T. Jones, and unbeknown to him, he had been living in an inexpensive hotel where there was another man with the name of Richard Jones, but with no middle initial.

A month before, Richard Jones (the man without the initial) walked out of the hotel and died on the sidewalk from a heart attack. His body was taken to the County Morgue, where a search of clothing was made for anything that would identify him.

In his pocket was found an unopened letter addressed to Richard T. Jones, the man I was talking with. A deputy coroner opened the letter, which had been written by the sister of Richard T. Jones. She lived in North Carolina. In the letter the sister explained that she had been paying the premiums on a life insurance policy.

The Coroner's Office notified the sister about the apparent death of her brother, and the insurance was collected to bury Richard Jones in a Chicago cemetery. Richard T. Jones did not know that he had been buried until a month or so later when his government pension check did not come through.

A trip to inquire about his pension at the Federal Building proved futile. He was told in no uncertain words that he was simply playing an old game, trying to collect a pension of a friend who had died.

"Nobody will believe that I am alive, and I don't have any money to live on," sobbed Richard T. Jones.

I forgot about all the routine assignments for the day and went to work checking out the story told by Richard T. Jones. I walked to the inexpensive hotel, which was nearby, where the desk clerk told me that he could have made the mistake of giving Richard T. Jones' letter to Richard Jones. I telephoned the Coroner's Office and the cemetery, and everything was as Richard T. Jones had told me.

City News reporters were not authorized to make long-distance telephone calls, which I very much needed to make. Richard T. Jones had shown me a birthmark, which left no doubt about who he was. It was a birthmark that would mean something to his sister in North Carolina. But I had no way to make the telephone call, until a detective sergeant at the station came to the rescue. He had overhead my telephone calls, and he said that he would make the phone call for me.

That is all that it took. Richard T. Jones was recalled to life, and with the detective sergeant's help, we were able to convince the federal pension office to restore Richard T. Jones to the active pension rolls.

I was way behind on my other work for City News that day, but fortunately I was redeemed by the fact that my story on Richard T. Jones being recalled to life made the front page of the newspapers the next morning.

It was the hectic time I spent at City News that proved to me what I really liked about journalism—the pleasure of reporting the things that strike the human chord.

Other City News Adventures. . .

CHAPTER 6

As a City News reporter I met the first and only gangster I was ever to know—except he was dead.

It also was the first and only time that I was authorized to take a taxicab as a City News reporter.

It happened at mid-afternoon on a warm, sunny day in June about three weeks after I had begun working at the City News Bureau. I was having an especially hectic day on the West Side police beat.

The city editor, Larry Mulay, told me to drop everything and grab a cab to get to the County Morgue as soon as possible.

"A gangster has been killed, and we are right on deadline for the late edition of the afternoon papers," said Mulay. "Take a look at the body and find out where he was shot and also give us a detailed description of the clothes he was wearing."

I had no idea where the County Morgue was because I had never been there before, but fortunately the cab driver knew.

After a five-minute ride, I got out at a small, two-story building on the south side of the large County Hospital. It was pretty hot, and the front door and most of the windows had been left open to help circulate the air.

I had heard that inquests and other activities at the morgue took place in the morning and that the afternoon was very quiet there. Even so, it was somewhat of a surprise to find how quiet it was.

There was no one there, not even an attendant at the information desk just inside the entrance. Knowing how important it was to get the information as quickly as possible, I went down an open stairway to the basement, being attracted by an unusual odor.

There he was—my first gangster acquaintance—on a slab covered by blood from head to toe. The body was identified by a nametag attached to a big toe.

I had found the right man, but I couldn't tell where he had been shot because of the blood covering the body. I was able to get a detailed description of his clothing, which was lying on a small table at the edge of the slab.

Returning to the first floor, I immediately called my office and was turning in the information to a rewrite man who interrupted with a question: "Where was this man shot?"

"I can't tell you," I replied. "The body is all covered with blood, and there is no one in the morgue to answer that question."

"Nobody in the morgue?" shouted the rewrite man. "I've heard about everything, but nothing as wild as this one. If you want your job, find out right away where he was shot and call me back."

Fortunately, just then the man in charge of the morgue returned from having had coffee at a nearby restaurant. He explained that the gangster had been shot mostly in the chest by a shotgun.

All of the newspapers in late afternoon and early morning editions told how the gangster, who was head of the Hod Carriers Union, had been killed on his way back from the racetrack. He had stopped at a stop-and-go light on Ogden Avenue, when a car pulled alongside and a man with the backseat window lowered fired at him.

The story was played on the front page under a top banner headline, and all the leads were similar to this one:

"A Chicago gangster, who was head of the Hod Carriers Union, was shot to death yesterday when he stopped at a stoplight on his way back from the races. He was wearing green silk underwear."

I was so elated I could hardly contain myself. Here was my first major achievement as a metropolitan journalist. The reference to "green silk underwear" was the information I had contributed as a City News reporter while determining where the gangster was shot.

My time at City News was many years before the advent of computer and electronic communications. The rewrite men in the City News Bureau typed on wax paper, which then was used in mimeograph machines for duplicating pages of news stories.

The Bureau had its headquarters on the seventh floor of the Ashland Block Building at the northeast corner of Randolph and Clark Streets, kitty-cornered from the County Building-City Hall. From the basement of the Ashland Block, the City News Bureau sent the stories in large bullet-like capsules through a pneumatic tube system to the various newspapers and to other major outlets, such as the County, Federal and the Board of Trade buildings.

Most of the City News pneumatic tubes were in the old tunnel system that had been dug many years ago in Chicago's downtown Loop, mainly to carry coal and ashes to and from the buildings.

For the newspapers, the pneumatic tube outlet at the Board of Trade Building was especially important because that was the place where pages of the early afternoon results from the New York and Chicago Stock Exchanges were relayed to the newspapers' financial news desks.

Once in a while, a prankster reporter in the County Building would catch a mouse and put it in one of the capsules and send it to his city desk, just to liven up the day. During World War II, the Board of Trade pneumatic tube was the conduit for a rather questionable practical joke.

The regular *Tribune* reporter at the Board of Trade had been able to find a good source for chewing gum, which, because of the war, was generally in short supply. As a special favor, this reporter every day sent a package of tablet-sized chewing gum through the tube to the editing desk of the *Tribune's* Financial News Department.

When the regular reporter went on vacation, his substitute was advised by the financial desk editors that he was expected to provide its daily supply of tablet-sized chewing gum. Unable to find a source for the gum, the substitute reporter concluded that there was more than one way to skin a cat.

He obtained a supply of a mild laxative in tablet form for the week that the regular reporter was away. He then sent each day a supply of tablets in chewing gum wrappers by way of the pneumatic tube to the financial news desk.

The editors had no idea what had hit them, but they thought that something was amiss. However, they still chewed the tablets each day. Some thought that they may have been eating too much fatty meat. Several who were in the custom of spending two or three hours each evening after work at a bar even went so far as to almost stop drinking before the week was over.

The perpetrator never did tell his victims what had actually happened, although he did tell me and several other trusted friends.

In my 60 years of journalism, the only time I was ever threatened with a libel suit was during my first year at City News Bureau. After six months of police reporting, I was assigned to the County Building to cover the civil courts.

It was there that I witnessed the dying days of Chicago's famous Front Page era, named for the play written by Ben Hecht and Charles MacArthur, both reporters in the 1920s.

It was a harum-scarum time when divorces and other scandals in private lives made big headlines. It was also a time when a few reporters who had grown old on bootleg gin during Prohibition still ruled the roost in press rooms, including the press room in the County Building. As a holdover from the front-page days of scandalous journalism, divorce stories got front page attention. Newspaper photographers often brought divorcées to the press room to take their pictures. One afternoon a photographer brought in a divorcée who was a striptease dancer by profession. Somebody helped her to get on top of a card table where she went into her act, taking almost everything off. At times like that, it was very difficult to be a reporter.

One photographer fell in love with a divorcée he had photographed. He ended up marrying her, and they apparently lived happily ever after. She had won a million-dollar settlement in the divorce, and her new photographer-husband, as a result, took an early retirement.

The pressroom on the fourth floor of the County Building was used by reporters covering the county government and the civil courts, including the divorce courts. The pressroom featured an open bar of gin, beer and whiskey, beginning at 8 o'clock in the morning and continuing until early evening. To keep out freeloaders, the old-timers of the pressroom kept the room locked at all times, and a reporter assigned to cover the County Building was issued a key so he could use the room.

The liquor was supplied by lawyers specializing in divorces, who were grateful for getting their cases with their names in the newspapers. Sometimes several of the older reporters who had been enjoying the bar since morning were pretty much out of it by early afternoon, and as a result, they asked the younger reporters to cover the cases in the courtrooms and give them the information.

Like other young reporters, I was happy to help them because their friendship could be very important in getting recommendations later for jobs on the newspapers. However, one day such cooperation almost cost me my job.

Covering a divorce hearing was very difficult because there was little or no record made of accusations that were flung between husbands and wives. During this particular hearing, the wife, almost at the top of her voice, accused her husband of using her best negligee to bed down his Irish setter, all of which I dutifully reported to the other reporters in the pressroom. The result was a small but highly noticeable story on the front page of the newspapers about an inconsiderate Oak Park doctor.

The doctor was so incensed that he called all of the newspapers and the City News Bureau and threatened to file libel suits. I was told to spend the day interviewing everyone in the courtroom to prove that what I reported was accurate.

When it was all over, the doctor must have had second thoughts about his libel threat. Behind the scenes, the older reporters for whom I was getting information took action. They may well have contacted the judge, for within a day or two the judge ruled in favor of the wife, giving her a large settlement.

One of the most rewarding pleasures of being a cub reporter at the City News Bureau was having experienced newspaper reporters as mentors and tutors.

Besides having reporters at the Central Police Station in downtown Chicago, the *Chicago Tribune* and the other papers also had police reporters covering the South, West, and North Sides, as well as the major suburbs.

Reporters were at the Central Police Station around the clock, and in the other parts of the city they usually worked 8-hour shifts during days or from 4 o'clock in the afternoon until midnight.

It was during the late afternoon and evening hours that I met the experienced reporters, usually on the South and West Sides. The *Tribune* reporters at that time were Newberne A. "Shadow" Browne, a kindly man with a remnant of a Southern accent; George Woltman, who later became an outstanding general assignment reporter; George Hartmann, later the *Tribune's* labor editor; and Al Krause, who later was the chauffeur and bodyguard for Don Maxwell, the editor.

As experienced reporters, the *Tribune* men knew how to get along with people and were very good friends with policemen, although they still kept their distance as newsmen should.

It was with George Woltman that I had my first experience of covering a murder. The scene was a front lawn of a modest house on the Northwest Side. An official of a printers' union had been killed by a shotgun blast in the front yard of his home. The murder apparently had been committed by a gangster of a mob that was trying to take over the printers' union.

As we got out of his car in front of the house, Woltman told me to go with him into the house, to keep my hat on, to say nothing and ask no questions, and simply act as if we belonged there. He said some of the policemen were bound to recognize him, but they wouldn't mind our being there as long as we did not interfere with their work.

After 15 minutes or so, George and I sat down on a sofa with the widow of the murdered man in between us. George was consoling the widow and at the same time getting information about the murdered man and his family. I looked at George and noticed that while he had his right arm around the widow's shoulder, he was reaching with his left hand under a stand at the side of the sofa, from which he took the family album.

It was not unusual—in fact it was expected—for reporters at murder scenes to steal photographs wherever possible. The newspapers would always send the photographs back the next day by a special messenger and with a thank-you note. George that night made off with the family album for the *Tribune*, which had exclusive pictures in the morning paper.

The important thing that George taught me, however, was that to be accepted at an unusual scene, the thing to do was to act as if one belonged there and not to ask questions or make any disturbance.   Meanwhile, one could learn everything that was going on.

It was a lesson that stood me in good stead a number of times later in my reporting work.

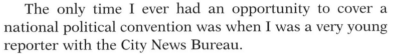

The only time I ever had an opportunity to cover a national political convention was when I was a very young reporter with the City News Bureau.

It was a July evening in 1940 when a deep-bass voice boomed out in the Chicago Stadium on Madison Street on the West Side.

"We want Roosevelt! We want Roosevelt! We want Roosevelt! We want Roosevelt!"

Tom Garry, the commissioner of sewers for the City of Chicago, was speaking over a microphone from the basement.

Garry had been assigned by the Chicago Democratic political organization to touch off what would appear to be a spontaneous demonstration on the floor of the Democratic National Convention for the nomination of President Franklin Delano Roosevelt to an unprecedented third term.

I was one of several City News reporters assigned to look for unusual feature stories at the convention. I was assigned to the first-floor corridor at the main entrance of the stadium on Madison Street.

At that time part of Madison Street was known as "Skid Row," a stretch of saloons and "flophouse" hotels catering to homeless men.

Just before the demonstration for Roosevelt was to begin, a large group of men from Skid Row came in the Madison Street entrance.

They were carrying large Roosevelt posters on long wooden handles, waving them about. As they flailed their posters, they broke overhead light fixtures and bulbs in the corridor. There was flying glass, but no one was hurt.

Policemen led the more enthusiastic demonstrators back through the doors to Madison Street. Others who had been more careful with their posters went inside to join the demonstration.

I learned that the Skid Row men had been recruited by Democratic party workers an hour or so earlier. Each had been paid 50 cents, the equivalent of two shots of cheap whiskey.

The payment in advance had proved to be a big mistake. Most of the men had immediately drunk up their earnings.

As a result of his performance at the convention, Tom Garry went down in history as the "Voice from the Sewer."

As a City News reporter in 1940, I survived six months of covering what was undoubtedly one of the hardest beats ever conceived in journalism—the civil courts in the Cook County Building in downtown Chicago. The courts had not yet been consolidated, and for one reason or another, there were two major courts very much alike, the Circuit Court and the Superior Court. In addition, there were a County Court, a Municipal Court, and a Probate Court (which had jurisdiction over estates).

Sheer luck was a critical factor as to whether one could be a successful City News reporter. It was luck in the first place to get a temporary summertime job. When three colleagues and I were hired in June of 1939, it was reported that more than 300 applicants had been turned down.

The new reporters had been hired in June to fill in for older staff members taking vacations, and we were told that our futures depended on whether there would be any vacancies after the vacation period.

In August of 1939, which was my first summer at City News, a crisis occurred which threatened everyone at the Bureau. One of the major supporters and part owner of City News, a morning newspaper named the *Herald-Examiner*, went out of business after a prolonged strike brought on by the newly organized newspaper editorial guild. With the loss of a supporting newspaper, the City News Bureau was forced to reduce its staff.

As one of the newest staff members, I felt that I had no hope of continuing with City News. On a Friday evening just before decisions were scheduled to be made on the reorganized staff, I was covering the police beat on the North Side.

Believing that I would no longer have a job, I took off two hours that evening to join a friend from Indiana at a nightclub and then came back to a police station at midnight to check out with the City News night desk. A veteran night editor, Joe Levandier, said that I couldn't leave until I had obtained the information on two stories that I had not done because of my absence and that had already appeared in the early newspaper editions.

"There's no point in my getting those stories," I told Levandier, "because I'm not going to be working at City News bureau any longer after this weekend."

Levandier replied, "Don't get in a hurry about that. No decisions have been made yet, and you might still be an employee come Monday morning. My advice is for you to clean up the night work that you missed before jumping to any conclusions."

It took me two hours to catch up on the work that night and to get permission from Levandier to go home.

About noon on Saturday, I received a telephone call from Ruby Ryan, the switchboard lady at City News, who was like a mother hen to all of us young reporters.

"No decisions have been made yet on the revised staff," said Ruby, "so sit by your phone until I call you sometime today or tomorrow to let you know what the situation will be."

Early Sunday evening, the telephone call came from Ruby.

"You will still be on the staff," Ruby said. "Check with the desk the first thing Monday morning to see what beat you will be working."

All of the new reporters, who were making the minimum salary of $20 a week, were kept on, while older reporters who were making twice or three times that much were let go.

During my second summer at City News, in 1940, a good friend and I.U. graduate, Leo Melzer, joined City News as a beginning reporter.

Leo was especially well qualified for the job because he had grown up in Gary and was well acquainted with the Chicago area. Knowing the city and the area is a requisite for being a good reporter.

Leo was also a good softball player. That was particularly important because our city editor, Larry Mulay, was coach of our softball team, which played in the evenings in Grant Park.

We were a group of tired players, having put in a hard day of work as reporters. Our opponents were husky young men from the circulation departments of the newspapers. With such competition, I don't think we won a single game during the summer.

Leo was our only good hitter, and had it not been for him, we would have been skunked all the time without ever having scored a run.

Despite his good reporting, Leo kept telling me that he felt he wouldn't be with City News Bureau after the softball season was over. I kept reassuring him by saying that he was as good if not better than anyone else and that he shouldn't worry.

But sure enough, when the season was over, Leo was let go on grounds that there were not enough vacancies to take care of all the summertime temporary employees.

Fortunately, Leo was able to get a job as a reporter for what was then a daily newspaper in Evanston, the *News-*

Index. Later, Leo became a reporter for the *Los Angeles Mirror*, and then for many years had a very successful career with the U.S. Information Agency.

While he was with the *Evanston News-Index*, Leo continued living with us at the home of my aunt, Grace Warne, on Chicago's Northwest Side. Also with us was another I.U. journalism graduate, Tom Miller, who was with the United Press and who later was sports information director for the I.U. Athletic Department.

One morning we woke up to find another I.U. journalism graduate, David B. Richardson, sitting on Aunt Grace's front steps. Dave had been hitchhiking from city to city looking for a job. Being very persistent, he later became a reporter for *Yank*, the World War II Army magazine, a foreign correspondent for *Time* and an editor of *U.S. News & World Report*.

Before World War II, the Chicago newspapers hired most of their new reporters from City News Bureau. When a reporter was needed, for instance, the *Tribune*, would ask for two or three prospects to be sent over for interviews.

As already indicated, one could have no better friend at City News than Ruby Ryan, the switchboard operator. Throughout the day, Ruby relayed assignments to reporters and could be very helpful in telling us about the ins and outs for success at City News. Listening in at the switchboard, Ruby was also well informed on everything that was going on with the management at City News.

"Drop everything for 15 or 20 minutes and go out and get a haircut," Ruby would tell a reporter. "You need to look your best because later this morning you will be told about going to the *Tribune* this afternoon for an interview."

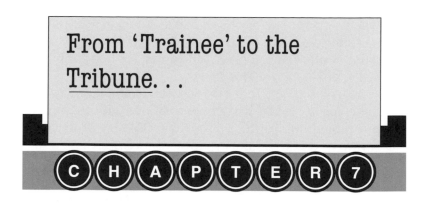

From 'Trainee' to the Tribune. . .

CHAPTER 7

September of 1940 was a major journalistic milestone for me.

That was when I was hired by the *Chicago Tribune*. After having spent 15 months as a cub reporter with the City News Bureau, I felt quite confident about becoming a *Tribune* reporter.

It was a big change, though, something very much like the difference between night and day.

City News had been a wonderful experience, but it also had been very hectic and stressful. From the very first day, one felt very much at home at the *Tribune*. It was like joining a friendly family.

I was assigned to the Financial News Department, and while I knew hardly anything at all about financial news, I felt very much at ease.

"Do you know the difference between a stock and a bond?" asked Philip Hampson, the assistant financial news editor.

I replied with some hesitation, "I'm not really sure."

"Don't worry about it because you'll learn in a hurry," said Hampson. "What we are looking for are not experts in finance, but good reporters who can report on any situation or subject."

As I was soon to learn, that was the keynote of the *Tribune* editorial staff. Reporters were hired not for their expertise in any given subject, but rather for their ability to report on any type of news story.

A week or so later, Tom Furlong, the financial news editor, gave me a special assignment. It was an assignment from Colonel McCormick himself—Colonel Robert R. McCormick, the well-known editor and publisher of the *Tribune.*

Colonel McCormick, who died in 1955 at the age of 75, was one of the last of the so-called giants in newspaper publishing. As editor and publisher of the *Chicago Tribune* for more than 30 years, he was a controversial conservative Republican whose views were reflected in outspoken editorials and Saturday evening talks he gave over the *Tribune's* radio station, WGN.

At the same time, he was highly patriotic, having served with the 1st Division in France in World War I. He developed the *Tribune* into one of the nation's largest newspapers, which hit a peak daily circulation of 1,074,000 in 1947. He was especially interested in technology and was a leader in the development of improvements in newspaper printing.

By making assignments, Colonel McCormick apparently was emulating his grandfather, Joseph Medill, at one time a major owner and editor of the *Tribune.* Medill had a practice of making assignments every day to his staff, and Colonel McCormick often did the same.

The Colonel was known to have had an interest in almost everything. It was said that he could look at a fence post and ask 10 interesting questions. At times, however, it was difficult for assignment editors to figure out exactly what the Colonel had in mind. Often, his assignments consisted of one phrase or one sentence without any further explanation.

The Colonel's assignments carried the special designation of "RRMC." The designation "RRMC" meant that everything had to be done to get some kind of a story.

In some instances, the assignments from Colonel McCormick turned out to be major stories. That was the case with the assignment given to me by Furlong as my first experience with a McCormick story.

From a report about ocean shipping, the Colonel had learned that one company had reduced the number of trips by freighters in the North Atlantic.

"What has happened to the freighters on the Atlantic?" read the assignment from the Colonel.

Furlong told me, "Spend the day telephoning large companies doing business overseas to find out what's happening, and then let me have a memo."

From the first telephone call, it was obvious what was happening. World War II had started in Europe a year earlier, in September of 1939, and the increasing activity of German submarines in the Atlantic was causing freight lines to cut down on their trips.

The next day Furlong also assigned two other financial reporters to make telephone calls, and by the end of the week we had accumulated a large amount of information of how the war in Europe was affecting world trade.

We all came down for an extra day of work on Saturday and turned our information over to an expert writer, George Morgenstern, who normally worked on the rewrite desk and later was chief editorial writer.

The story about freighters on the Atlantic appeared in the *Tribune* on Monday morning. It turned out to be the first story to be done in this country on how the European war was seriously affecting the American economy. The story began on the front page with a column and the top headline, and was continued for a full page inside. It was an excellent example of how an assignment by Colonel McCormick could produce an important story.

Dick Orr, the *Tribune* farm editor, had a large collection of assignments from the Colonel, who used part of his Cantigny Estate in DuPage County as an experimental farm. As farm editor, Orr received a constant flow of assignments from the Colonel. Many of the Colonel's assignments resulted in interesting stories, but, Orr said, some made little or no sense.

For instance, in one of his assignments to Orr, the Colonel suggested that scientists develop chickens that would lay only double-yolk eggs, all of which, he said, would result in greater food production.

Walter Trohan, who filled one of the most prestigious positions at the *Tribune,* as head of the Washington Bureau, had great admiration for Colonel McCormick as an editor, although Trohan said the Colonel could do "some of the damnedest things at times."

"For instance, just before World War II he sent me an assignment that he had scrawled on a piece of newspaper," Trohan recalled.

"The assignment simply was: 'Fix Europe.'

"That was all it said. That was an assignment one obviously couldn't do anything about. But in most instances, there was some way or another that one could take action and end up with a reasonable story."

Before we met, my wife (whose maiden name was Ruth Moss) was editor of the *Tribune's* employee monthly magazine, known as *The Little Trib.*

Ruth was surprised and puzzled when she received this note from Colonel McCormick:

"Miss Moss-

Kissing a man without a mustache is like eating an egg without salt.

(Signed)

McC"

"I knew something should be done," recalled Ruth. "The question was what?

"Then I thought about it for a while and I thought, 'A-ha!' "

Ruth felt she had a good answer for the Colonel. From the reference room she obtained photographs of Colonel McCormick, who had a mustache, and eight other *Tribune* men with mustaches.

For *The Little Trib*, Ruth had a layout artist design one page showing only the mustaches of the Colonel and the eight other men. At the top of the display was a headline: "Can You Identify These Men By Their Mustaches?"

In boldface letters at the bottom of the display, readers were advised to turn to the next page for answers.

The second page showed full headshots of Colonel McCormick and the others with the mustaches. Under that display in large italic letters was the single quotation: "Kissing a man without a mustache is like eating an egg without salt."

Colonel McCormick, who often appeared without any notice in the City Room, was the subject of many amusing stories. Unfortunately, no one made a collection of these stories, which even the Colonel, who had a good sense of humor, would have probably enjoyed.

Here are a few more that I remember hearing about:

In the early years of aviation, the *Tribune*, at the direction of Colonel McCormick, sponsored a flight to the North Pole with a crew of explorers on board. A day or so after the flight took off, all contact with the plane was lost. It was assumed that the plane had crashed somewhere.

Anxious to find out what had happened, Colonel McCormick left word with the editors at the City Desk that he was to be contacted immediately, regardless of the hour, if and when word was received about the flight.

Late one night about a week later, word came through that a crash landing had been made to the north of the Hudson Bay area. Fortunately, everyone had survived with little or no injury, and they had been rescued by Eskimos. On duty as the night editor, Manly S. Mumford immediately got the *Tribune's* chief telephone operator on the wire and asked that she find out where he could contact the Colonel. Ten minutes went by, and Mumford became more and more anxious.

Finally, the chief telephone operator called Mumford and said that she had located the Colonel. Assuming that the operator was holding the Colonel on another line, Mumford blurted out, "In what shack did you find him tonight?"

To Mumford's great chagrin, the Colonel was on the same line and said, "In my Lake Forest shack—where else?" Then, to Mumford's relief, the Colonel punctuated his response with a burst of laughter.

Another story about the Colonel pertained to a complicated job of editing on the financial news copy desk. The job, which took about an hour and a half and had to be completed by a 3 o'clock deadline, involved the handling of page after page of reports of the stock and commodity markets and other financial news operations of the day.

Besides the sheets of market prices, one had to be certain that numerous other bits of information, such as the cotton price from Memphis and the turpentine price from Florida, were sent promptly to the third floor for typesetting. It was a hectic job that was done strictly by rote with no comprehension of what the markets had actually done.

One day the job was being done by one of our women copy editors, Minnie Wolf. She had just finished and was leaning back in her chair when she heard a deep voice.

"What, young lady, did the market do today?" asked the Colonel.

"It closed, Colonel—it closed," replied Miss Wolf, who had no idea of the closing prices of the market.

Some of the stories about Colonel McCormick involved his English bulldog, which was named Buster Boo.

Despite its pugnacious appearance, Buster Boo was a well-behaved and friendly dog, which the Colonel often brought to Tribune Tower.

Usually, when they saw him enter the lobby, people stood back to let the Colonel have an elevator to himself so that he could get directly to his office on the 24th floor. The elevator also had a stop for the fourth floor.

Early one evening, a copy boy had gone down to the first floor to buy an O'Henry candy bar and, after getting on an elevator to return, had just unwrapped it and had taken a bite when the Colonel got on with Buster Boo.

Being polite, the copy boy held the candy bar behind him; by the time he reached the fourth floor and got off, the O'Henry bar had disappeared. Buster Boo seemed to be licking his lips.

When the copy boy returned to the City Desk, he was asked what happened to the candy bar. After he told how Buster Boo had eaten the bar, someone got word up to the Colonel's office—and a nickel was sent down to the copy boy for a new bar.

Another incident involving Buster Boo was a story about a *Tribune* photographer taking photos of guests at a dinner party given by Colonel McCormick and then, at the invitation of the Colonel, joining the guests at the dinner table.

It was such a delicate assignment that the *Tribune's* assistant chief photographer, Al Madsen, was chosen. Madsen was a polished and well-mannered man, who could be expected to handle the assignment with perfect aplomb.

However, even he had some doubts, so he sought advice from the editor, Don Maxwell.

"Do you have any ideas of how I should act?" asked Madsen.

Maxwell replied, "Just do what the Colonel does."

It turned out to be a turkey dinner, and the Colonel heaped his plate with turkey and all the trimmings.

Madsen did the same, serving himself with generous portions of turkey, mashed potatoes, dressing and the like.

As other guests were served, the Colonel then put his plate on the floor, and said, "Here, Buster Boo."

Al Chase, who was a longtime real estate editor of the *Tribune*, and his wife, Audrey, had a farm near Glen Ellyn in DuPage County, and they annually hosted a late Sunday afternoon picnic in September for the financial news staff.

In the summer they lived in a screened-in house in the center of a 43-acre cornfield the Chases owned. The house was reached by a narrow dirt road which was hard to find when the corn was ready for harvest.

For their annual financial news picnic, the Chases had always invited the McCormicks but they had never come— that is, until that Sunday afternoon in 1946.

"Daddy, is that Colonel McCormick?" asked the 6-year-old daughter of one of our financial news reporters.

Sure enough, it was Colonel McCormick and Mrs. McCormick. There had been a cracking sound as they had parted corn stalks to get to the Al Chase picnic.

Colonel and Mrs. McCormick had not been able to find the road; so they had walked through the cornfield to get to the picnic site—and fortunately did not get even more lost.

"I'm sorry you had to walk through the cornfield," said Al. "But it's great to have you with us. We'll be eating pretty soon, so meanwhile we can all sit down and have a visit."

Al had just repainted his outdoor furniture in the patriotic colors of red, white and blue.

The Colonel selected a large metal chair with armrests that had been painted red. A half-hour or so later, when everyone got up for dinner, there was suddenly total silence. Even the youngest children were quiet. You could have heard a pin drop in the grass.

The Colonel was standing still, apparently not knowing exactly what to do. Red paint had come off on the seat of his light-colored pants and on the sleeves of his summer coat.

In such a situation, most *Tribune* men probably would just have had their heart attack right then and called it quits. But not Al Chase.

"I'm sorry, Colonel," said Al. "But I think I can take that paint out with some high-test cleaning fluid I have in the well-house."

The Colonel, who was always interested in technological challenges, said, "You think you can, Al?"

"Just come with me," said Al as he began leading the Colonel to the well-house.

It was quite a sight: The Colonel, who was 6 feet 4 inches tall, following Al, who was not much taller than 5 feet.

Mrs. McCormick helped to break the silence.

"I've been telling him he should throw that old suit away," she said.

In 15 minutes, the Colonel and Al reappeared, and everyone joined the line for the covered dish dinner. All of the paint was gone from the Colonel's coat and pants.

Al was one of the few editorial people at the *Tribune* who felt perfectly at home with the Colonel. Whenever he got an assignment from the Colonel that was not clear, Al did not hesitate to go up to the 24th floor and ask the Colonel to clarify the assignment.

The following story was told to me by Wayne Thomis, the *Tribune's* aviation editor and all-around reporter. During a 40-year career with the paper, Thomis was one of the most versatile and talented reporters and writers in the *Tribune's* history.

For a time I had the pleasure of sitting beside him in the City Room. He was very personable and he always attacked every story with the utmost enthusiasm.

Colonel McCormick had his own pilots for his airplane, but he liked Thomis so much that he often asked Wayne to be his pilot. Wayne told me that one of his most unusual trips piloting the Colonel was to Cuba in the 1950s.

The Colonel had arranged to have an early evening dinner with the ruler of Cuba at that time, Fulgencio Batista. Wayne said he was surprised that the Colonel had any interest in Batista, who was generally known as a tyrant.

The scheduling of the dinner date for the Colonel involved a lot of effort, with the *Tribune* having to go to the U.S. State Department for help.

When they landed in Havana in the early afternoon, the Colonel told Wayne to stand by at the airport and be available by telephone. They were to fly back to Chicago later that evening, after the dinner.

To Wayne's surprise, the Colonel called about 4 o'clock and said to have the plane ready for a takeoff as soon as he got there.

It wasn't until they were well on their way home that the Colonel gave an explanation of their early return. The Colonel said that he had called Batista's office and explained that he would have to forego their dinner date because he had forgotten about a conflicting engagement in Chicago.

I remember Wayne saying, "This all boiled down to one thing. It was the Colonel's way of showing complete contempt for Batista."

The era of speechmaking as a major source of news began during the 1930s "New Deal" administration of President Franklin D. Roosevelt.

In his radio fireside chats, President Roosevelt communicated directly to the people about his policies and new programs. Members of the cabinet and other federal government officials also gave speeches throughout the country on the government's policies.

In response, leaders of business and industry often spoke out about the government policies, either in favor or in opposition. The government speeches also provided material for comment by newspapers in their editorials.

At the *Tribune*, the Roosevelt policies often were attacked in editorials because of Colonel McCormick's opposition to President Roosevelt. There was little, if anything, that the Roosevelt Administration did that pleased McCormick.

As air travel developed, Chicago became the nation's aviation center, and government officials from Washington frequently had to stop over briefly to make flight connections.

In the fall of 1940, as a newly hired reporter, I was sent by the *Tribune's* financial editor to Midway Airport to interview Dean Acheson, a top official in the Roosevelt Administration. Acheson was scheduled to make a talk on farm policy that evening in Des Moines, Iowa. My assignment was to get a copy of his speech or a short interview during a layover of 45 minutes or so at Midway Airport.

I was able to approach Acheson just as he had stepped off the plane, but I had no more than identified myself as a *Tribune* reporter before Acheson stalked off, saying, "I don't have any time for the *Chicago Tribune*."

Just then someone tapped me on the shoulder and, upon turning around, I recognized Nelson Rockefeller, who was traveling with Acheson.

"Let's have a cup of coffee," Rockefeller said to me.

I had a feeling that Rockefeller wanted to get away from the Acheson group for a bit. We took stools at the coffee counter and, to make conversation, I asked Rockefeller what he was doing with Acheson and the government.

He explained that he was getting a new appointment in the State Department as a special U.S. representative in South American affairs.

I asked if it would be all right for me to interview him and make some notes. He said that the appointment had not been announced yet, but there was no reason why he couldn't tell me what he was planning to do.

Back in the office, I told our financial editor, Tom Furlong, what had happened, and he told me to write as much as I wanted about Rockefeller and his new appointment as a State Department representative for South American affairs. From my interview with Nelson Rockefeller, I wrote more than 1,200 words.

At that time, the *Chicago Tribune* and *The New York Times* had a daily practice of exchanging news stories. Each paper had a reporter in the City Room of the other newspaper to choose and send whatever stories were considered important.

The New York Times representative in the *Tribune's* City Room was a very friendly reporter by the name of Luther Horne, whom we called Trader Horne. In writing major stories, the *Tribune* reporters always made an extra carbon copy for Trader to pick up and send by wire to *The Times* in New York.

Exchange stories did not carry bylines but rather a designation of "Special to The New York Times" or "To the Chicago Tribune."

The next morning, however, I was happy to see that *The New York Times* had used everything I had written as a lead story on the front page.

Whatever Dean Acheson said that evening in Des Moines was lost and overshadowed by this story about Nelson Rockefeller.

My time in the Financial News Department continued for about nine months before it was interrupted in June 1941. Six months before Pearl Harbor, I was drafted into the Army.

In the Service of Uncle Sam

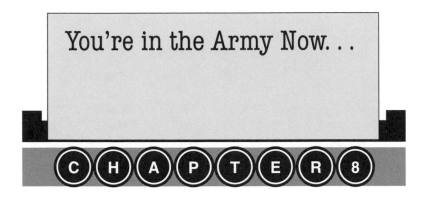

You're in the Army Now...

C H A P T E R 8

The year 1941 was a time when the very young and very healthy men were drafted by their Selective Service Boards for one year of military service.

In June as a draftee, I went off to the Army by streetcar. It was an Army-chartered streetcar that picked up 60 of us draftees at 8 o'clock in the morning at Montrose and Milwaukee Avenues on Chicago's Northwest Side. That was less than a block from where I had been living in the home of Aunt Grace.

Besides a shaving kit and a change of socks and underwear, I took with me my portable Corona typewriter. It must have been a journalistic instinct.

The streetcar took us to downtown Chicago by way of Milwaukee Avenue and then west of the Loop two miles on Madison Street to a National Guard Armory.

One fellow draftee was so drunk he could hardly get on the streetcar. He carried a small black bag, which fell open, spilling its contents, three ripe bananas, on the floor. That was all he was taking—no shaving kit or any other personal items, just three ripe bananas.

Two of our group helped him into the Armory. But when a sergeant ordered us to line up, they had to let go of him, and our drunken draftee fell flat on his face. That was the last we saw of him as he was carried away. For all we know, he could well have kept sober thereafter and ended up winning the Congressional Medal of Honor for exceptional bravery in action. Such things, we learned later, could happen in the Army.

At the National Guard Armory we were given physical examinations and then hustled off by bus to the North Western Station for a train ride to Camp Grant near Rockford.

We spent the next two days at the Reception Center at Camp Grant being processed as "unqualified privates." The important part of that process was an interview about our capabilities. The highlights of our background and capabilities were recorded in the form of punches on the edges of a rectangular personnel card, which was to be used to indicate the type of service to which we could be assigned.

Some of the unqualified privates in our group were sent to Hawaii, where six months later they were to be among the American troops bombed in the Japanese attack at Pearl Harbor.

The more fortunate of us went by troop train to a new infantry training post, Camp Wolters, near Mineral Wells, Texas. The small city of Mineral Wells, about 50 miles west of Ft. Worth, was known as the "Home of Crazy Water Crystals," which could be better described as rotten-egg-smelling sulfur water.

There were 800 of us in the 51st Infantry Training Battalion, four companies of 200 each. We were in a brand new section of the camp, and we spent the first two weeks building sidewalks of crushed white stone.

It was very hot during the day, sometimes getting up to 110 degrees. But the nights were quite comfortable, usually fanned by a cool breeze.

Strange as it may sound, being in an infantry training battalion as an unqualified private was a carefree existence compared to being a competitive journalist. Although Army training at times could be tiring, one felt relaxed because there was nothing else to do but to relax and enjoy it.

Most of one's needs were taken care of. For an "unqualified private" the pay was $21 a month, from which one first had to deduct $3 for the monthly laundry bill. The Post Exchange (PX) was very inexpensive. A milkshake, for instance, cost only 10 cents. The only alcoholic beverage available was 3.2 beer, which was supposed to be weak; but in the hot Texas weather, it could deliver a good punch.

Shortly before I was drafted, an older friend who had served in World War I told me that one should never volunteer for anything in the Army—a bit of advice I took very much to heart.

Our first sergeant at Camp Wolters was a long-time enlisted man and a man of very few words. He used a whistle to have us "fall in" and "fall out."

One Friday morning after we had "fallen in," he made a special announcement.

"I need volunteers for special duty," he said without giving any explanation.

Six men stepped forward—six "stupid" men, or so the rest of us thought.

"Okay," said our sergeant, "you six volunteers get your clean uniforms on and be ready in a half hour to leave for Denton. Be on your best behavior because you're going to be guests for the weekend at the Denton Teachers College.

"The rest of you soldiers fall out here again in a half hour to start building some more sidewalks."

So much for the advice of the old soldier from the first World War!

At Camp Wolters I immediately put my portable Corona typewriter to good use.

We had a company of 200 interesting men. Nearly everyone had at least one college degree, and some had several degrees, including two with Ph.D. degrees.

I learned there was a public relations office at the camp headquarters. Without contacting that office, I began writing short personality sketches of our men and sending the sketches to the public relations office for forwarding to newspapers in the Chicago area. I tried to get a little feature twist into every profile.

I remember one sketch in particular because it was about a man who had the poorest eyesight in the company but turned out to be the best sharpshooter on the rifle range.

After two weeks or so, I knew that my articles were getting through to Chicago papers because Aunt Grace sent me clippings. She noticed the stories because Camp Wolters was mentioned. The newspapers apparently used almost anything that pertained to military life because of the public's interest in the drafting and training of men by the Army.

So I kept on writing, sending through at least a dozen articles a week to the public relations office.

One day a staff car came up, stopped at our company headquarters building, and the driver announced that he was looking for Private Buck, who was wanted at the camp headquarters. The first reaction by our company commander and first sergeant was an assumption that I had done something wrong, being guilty possibly of a criminal act. It was unusual, to say the least, to have a staff car arrive from camp headquarters to pick up an "unqualified private."

At the camp headquarters I was taken to the public relations office where I met the director, a major who formerly had been an editor for the *Cleveland Plain Dealer*. He explained that I had been doing excellent work by writing the personality sketches. He asked, however, that I slow down a little because his office had to make eight copies of everything I sent.

Even at a slower pace, I was able to write a short personality sketch about almost everyone in our company during the three months we were in basic training.

From Camp Wolters I was sent to Fort Custer, Michigan, near Kalamazoo, where I became a private first class making $36 a month. I was assigned to interview draftees at the Reception Center.

At Fort Custer I had the good fortune of becoming acquainted with a very good journalist, Stanley Swinton, who had been a reporter with the Associated Press in Detroit. Swinton was working in the public relations office of the Reception Center, and I began helping him in my spare time.

Our main project was producing a one-hour variety show every Friday evening to be broadcast over a Kalamazoo radio station. The show featured an Army dance band.

Besides helping to write the script, I also gave the news on the program. I began my newscast with this greeting:

"Hello, Mom. This is your Fort Custer fort-caster."

We had one problem. The major who was in charge of public relations at the Reception Center had been a politician in Michigan and still wished to get his name before the public. He insisted on being the main announcer for our variety shows. The trouble was, he lisped—lisped very badly.

As a result, Stan Swinton and I took turns week by week sitting with a portable typewriter across the desk from the major in his office. We would type a line for the script and hand it to the major to see if he could read it. If he lisped, we tried another line. By the time our show went on the air Friday night, we had a lisp-proof script for the major.

Even though Stan and I were enjoying ourselves at Fort Custer, we wanted to do something else. We kept watching the bulletin board for possible opportunities, and one day we saw a notice about a new investigation unit the Army was creating in Chicago. We sent in our applications, explaining that as former newspapermen, we felt that we could be good investigators.

Within a week, we were accepted and received orders to report to a Captain Elmer Michael Walsh of the Provost

Marshal's Office in Chicago. We telephoned Captain Walsh about our plans to arrive by train, and he met us at the station.

From there he took us directly to the Bonds clothing store on Madison Street in the Loop. We then went through the store, picking out two suits each, topcoats, hats and everything else needed for civilian dress.

From the clothing store, Captain Walsh took us to the Provost Marshal's Office, which was in the Civic Opera Building at 20 N. Wacker Drive. We were given desks and, of all things, assigned a secretary.

Captain Walsh explained that we were being promoted to staff sergeants and would be given an allowance to live wherever we chose. I returned to Aunt Grace's home, from which I would take a Milwaukee Avenue streetcar to and from downtown.

Our job was to make loyalty investigations of people who were to have sensitive positions with the military during the war. Many of the people we investigated were men who were to serve in the Signal Corps or the intelligence units. We also made loyalty checks on reporters for whom newspapers were seeking credentials for assignments as war correspondents.

In our investigations, we paid special attention to possible police records and memberships in anti-American organizations. In Chicago we had access to the files of newspaper offices and to records at the Chicago Police Department of what was called the "Red Squad," a special unit investigating people associated with Communist organizations.

For most of the cases, we started with information that had been given on application forms. However, in some cases, we had little more than the person's name, address, and place of work.

I once was given only a name of a person with the information that he was associated with an organization called the "United States Research Committee" at the University of Chicago.

Going to the U. of C. campus in Hyde Park on the South Side, I found that the United States Research Committee was housed in a nondescript two-story building.

Dressed as a civilian, I entered the front door without being stopped or questioned and was spending a lot of time talking with people at their desks and in the cafeteria about the man I was investigating.

Suddenly, I was grabbed by the nape of the neck by a police officer. He was none too gentle as he pushed me along the hall and into an office.

"What are you doing here?" asked an official-looking man behind a desk.

I identified myself and explained that I was making an investigation for the Provost Marshal's Office.

Without asking whom I was investigating, the man said, "Get out of here and don't come back."

The policeman showed me out the front door.

I completed the investigation by other means, but I never did learn exactly the purpose of the United States Research Committee.

That is, until the United States dropped the two bombs on Japan in August of 1945.

No wonder the official-looking man behind the desk had become so excited. Without being challenged, I had entered the ultra-secret sanctum of atomic research known as the Manhattan Project.

In no time at all, more than 50 soldier-investigators were assigned to the provost marshal's investigation unit. Most of the investigators had been lawyers, and, for the most part, they considered the assignment ideal, largely because they were still in the Army while leading a normal civilian life. All of the investigators held the rank of staff sergeant.

Some of us, however, still had a yearning for regular Army duty; and we believed the best way to do that was to go to an officers' school.

In the fall of 1942, several of us went to military police officers' school, which was at an Army post in Chickamauga Park near Chattanooga, Tennessee. Ironically, halfway through the 90-day officers' course, our school was moved to snowbound Fort Custer, Michigan, where I had spent the winter before as a private. After being commissioned a second lieutenant, I also took an extra 30-day course in occupational police work at the Fort Custer officers' school.

Much to my delight, I then was assigned to a military police battalion in San Francisco. Our company lived at the Presidio, the picturesque old Army post on the San Francisco Bay next to the Golden Gate Bridge. As a second lieutenant, I supervised military policemen who were on duty in the city, mostly in the areas of the nightclubs.

Eight months later I was transferred to a military government school at the University of Pittsburgh—an assignment that resulted from my having taken the course in occupational police work at Fort Custer. We lived in Hotel Webster Hall and had classes in a university building of Gothic architecture similar to Tribune Tower in Chicago. The military government school lasted for four months, with much of the instruction devoted to the German language. We studied oral German at least four hours a day.

At age 26, another second lieutenant and I were the youngest in the class. The other much older members had been outstanding in civilian life as lawyers, teachers, doctors, public health officials, city managers and other government officials. Some had served in World War I, which gave them the nickname of "Retreads."

Early in January of 1944, our military government class went to England on the *Ile de France*, a former luxury liner converted to a troop ship. It took only six days to sail from New York City to the Firth of Clyde in Scotland, near Glasgow. The *Ile de France* was so fast that it did not need the protection of a convoy.

The night before we sailed for England, the party telephone system in my hometown of Star City, Indiana, provided a unique service for me when I telephoned my mother.

After standing in line to use an outdoor telephone I called our Star City switchboard operator, Cora Hatfield. She operated the local telephone system which consisted of lines that were shared by groups of customers.

Unable to arouse my mother, Mrs. Hatfield said, "Thomas, I think your mother must be sleeping on her good ear tonight. I will wake up Sylvia Geier and have her go over and get your mother up to answer the phone."

Sylvia was our next-door neighbor and she had no difficulty getting into our house to rouse my mother because no one in Star City ever locked his doors in those years.

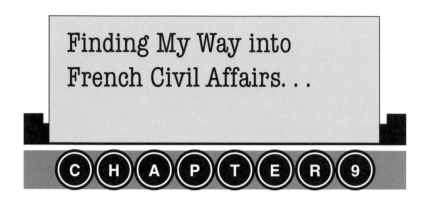

Finding My Way into French Civil Affairs. . .

CHAPTER 9

In England we became residents of very comfortable brick barracks at a British military post near Swindon, about 75 miles west of London. In the few remaining months before D-Day, these barracks became the temporary home for a large number of American, British and Canadian officers, all of whom were awaiting assignments in civil affairs or military government.

Our work, which consisted of an undefined variety of activities, was known as civil affairs in Allied countries, such as France, and military government in enemy countries, such as Germany.

It became so boring just sitting around with nothing to do that I finally volunteered to do office work. I was assigned as the secretary for a panel of three colonels who were selecting personnel for the various detachments of civil affairs and military government.

There were four sizes of detachments which were designated by the capital letters of A, B, C and D. The D detachment, which was the smallest, consisted of four officers and six GIs. The A, B, and C detachments were to serve in the larger towns and cities while the D detachments were to be very mobile and attached to the combat divisions, moving along as the war progressed.

After I had served as their secretary for six weeks, the colonels on the panel, apparently pleased with my work, asked what I would like to do and if they could help me.

I said that I would like not only to serve on a D detachment scheduled to go to France as early as possible, but also to select the commanding officer for that detachment. With the permission of the colonels, I made myself a junior officer member of Detachment D2G1 and selected an American major, George Viault, as the commanding officer. The Army's plan showed that our D2G1 detachment would be one of the first civil affairs units to land in France and that we possibly would be there on D-Day.

I knew Major Viault by sight, but I had never talked with him and did not know anything about him, except what I

World War II saw Tom Buck (right) serving in France as part of a special civil affairs detachment. Here he is shown with the detachment commander, Maj. George Viault.

had seen on his personnel record. He had been a federal government employee for more than 10 years, his most recent work having been with the Bureau of the Budget in Washington, D.C.

What really caught my eye, however, was that he was of French descent and was very fluent in French. I felt that he would be a wonderful commanding officer to serve with in France because of his knowledge of the French language and French people. For me, his affection and understanding of the French people proved to be the high point during the more than one year we served together in France.

As D2G1, we arrived at Omaha Beach on D plus 16, or June 22. We would have been there sooner had it not been for several heavy storms that occurred almost immediately after D-Day.

As it turned out, however, our service was not needed for more than a month by the 29th Infantry Division to which we had been assigned. We were held in reserve in the small town of Lison, where we occupied the public school building. Meanwhile, we gave whatever help we could to the mayor of Lison and his canton.

On July 14, which the French celebrate as Bastille Day, the mayor of Lison asked if we could help him with a special celebration. He said that he and the citizens of Lison wanted to show their appreciation for everything that the American Army was doing.

He said that Lison had a hidden supply of good wine to be shared with American soldiers, and he asked that we extend a general invitation to all the soldiers in the area.

From early morning until early evening on Bastille Day, the Lison mayor was the host at the reception, which was enjoyed by a constant flow of GIs and officers.

As the reception came to an end, the mayor, who was in his 70s, looked so tired that I suggested we give him a ride in our jeep to his home on the other side of town.

"No, I couldn't possibly let you do that," said the mayor. "If I let you take me home in your car, my people would think that I was drunk."

The mayor then set out on his own, walking slowly and staggering now and then from one side of the street to the other.

Our D2G1 detachment was held in reserve in Lison for most of July. We had so little to do that we felt more like tourists than soldiers. Our detachment had two Jeeps which we used for sightseeing. One day we took a trip to the quaint city of Bayeux, famous for its Bayeux tapestry telling the history of the Norman Conquest. Bayeux is also famous for its Camembert cheese. In driving around, we had to be very careful because there was no front line or anything indicating where the German army was.

On the morning of July 25 from a hill about 10 miles away, we witnessed a four-hour bombing by wave after wave of American bombers. It was a bombing that preceded the breakthrough by our army at St. Lo. It was also a bombing in which some bombs dropped short, resulting in the death of American soldiers, including Lieutenant General Leslie J. McNair, who had made a special inspection trip from Washington, D.C.

The Army reported later that the "short" bombing error killed 111 GIs and wounded 490. Fifteen hundred bombers of the Eighth Air Force dropped 3,400 tons of bombs.

On July 30, a few days after the breakthrough, we received our first assignment. We took over a refugee collection camp near Le Mesnil Herman, about 20 miles beyond St. Lo. A large vacant chateau with two barns had been taken over for the refugee camp.

During our tourist-like stay at Lison we had become somewhat nonchalant about the dangers of war. We had never thought about the necessity of foxholes even though late at night a German plane would always fly over. Because of its timing, it became known as "Bed Check Charlie" and was considered to be of little or no danger.

Foxholes were far from our minds the afternoon we arrived at the refugee camp—that is, until several infantry-men from a nearby field came over to tell us we were in a combat zone, and that we should be digging foxholes.

Taking that advice, some of us who didn't speak French too well went to work "digging in" while others of our detachment—those who spoke French fluently—tackled the problem of organizing some 200 refugees, providing food for them and assigning them to sleeping quarters.

At midnight, all was quiet except for the drone of a German plane.

"It must be 'Bed Check Charlie,'" someone said.

On many other nights we had never been too concerned about the late-night German plane because it was always quite distant from us. But this night it seemed to be directly overhead, so we jumped into our foxholes which we had dug in the orchard.

Two of our GIs and I had dug one hole so large that it easily accommodated our British major, one GI and myself along with a small stray dog that appeared from nowhere.

The plane first dropped flares that made everything so bright that I felt that, as a target, I was standing stark naked on a sun-lit hill. Next came incendiary bombs that set the thatch roofs of the two small barns on fire.

As he stepped from our hole, the British major said he thought we should try to put out the fires. I said I thought we should stay in the hole until we were sure the raid was over. Our GI decided to follow the major.

The GI had taken only a step or two before he was hit by shrapnel from one of the anti-personnel bombs the plane was dropping in the third pass over us. Our soldier had been hit in the right leg, and I pulled him back into our hole.

Two of our other GIs also had been hit by shrapnel after they were forced out of a foxhole they were sharing when their blankets caught fire from the spray of an incendiary bomb.

One of the soldiers got to the protection of a ditch at the side of the orchard on his own. But the other soldier, in apparent panic, stood as if he were frozen near the flaming foxhole. I ran to him and pulled him across the orchard and into the ditch.

Fortunately, for our three wounded GIs, there was an Army field hospital in tents directly across the road from us. It had not been a target of the bombing.

A mother, a three-year-old daughter and her infant died near the chateau from injuries received during the raid. None of the other refugees was injured.

The next morning our D2G1 detachment re-established the refugee camp at a nearby farmhouse and continued to operate there for the next week, taking care of 200 to 300 refugees daily. In moving the refugees to safe areas, we appealed to nearby Army units for use of their trucks.

As a small detachment, we moved from one small village to another as the 29th Division moved forward. Even though it might be for only one day, we would set up an office in the center of the village and put up posters to inform residents of our presence and our offer to help. We also would immediately contact the mayor and his secretary, as well as other leading citizens, including the police chief, the doctor, the priest and the proprietor of the pharmacy. If there were a hospital, we would also make our presence known and offer to help.

There was no rulebook for civil affairs and military government work, but our general objective was to keep the civilian population out of the way of the Army and to help civilians with their emergency needs. Often, we would use our two jeeps to help the farmers get their sacks of wheat to the mill.

For the Army, we were always concerned about keeping major routes free of carts and farm equipment. Once in a while, Major Viault and I would receive an assignment to make certain that major routes were clear of civilian traffic early in the morning so that Army units could move forward. Beginning about 4 a.m., each of us would take a jeep and a driver and begin contacting farmers along the routes.

That duty, however, did have one danger. The farmers wanted to thank us as Americans for liberating them and insisted that we have a toast of cognac or calvados with them. By breakfast, Major Viault and I would be feeling no pain.

It was a rare occasion for us to have any direct contact with the Germans. Once in Normandy, our detachment arranged to have four German prisoners taken to a prisoner-of-war camp after their presence had been brought to our attention by a French farmer.

The German soldiers, who apparently were deserters, had been helping the farmer harvest wheat. When the wheat was cut, the farmer had no further use for them; but they insisted on staying because they liked the home cooking.

Later, in the Brest area at the western end of the Brittany peninsula, I had another encounter with German soldiers. A British officer, Captain Dennis G. Greig, and I were assigned to handle civil affairs in a combat zone in Lambezellec, a suburb immediately north of Brest. We lived and had our office on the first floor of a brewery, with a high hill giving protection from fire from street fighting in Brest. The mayor of Lambezellec and his staff also had offices in the building, and in the basement our Army had a prisoner-of-war collecting point.

About 4 o'clock one morning, Captain Greig and I were awakened by the loud sound of what seemed to be a wild party.

Going to the basement, we found that several German soldiers had been brought in by our military policemen. The Germans had not been disarmed of their rifles and hand grenades, and instead of taking them on to a prison-of-war camp, our military policemen had invited them to help enjoy a keg of beer they had stolen from the brewery.

With no qualms about breaking up the beer-drinking party of Americans and Germans, we got help immediately from an Army regimental headquarters to have the German prisoners taken into custody.

Another incident in the Brest area involved taking special action to rein in a group of 30 Russian soldiers who had been terrorizing the countryside. They were anti-Communist or "white" Russians who had been fighting with the German army at Brest.

When they realized the battle at Brest was turning against the Germans, the Russians deserted the Germans and joined our American Army. When the battle at Brest was over and most of our Army had left, the Russian soldiers stayed behind. They took over a vacant chateau and began demanding food from French farmers at pistol point. We had our D2G1 office in the village of St. Renan, and the Russian soldiers came to our attention after they had caused a lot of trouble one Saturday night in a brothel.

On our own, we first tried to persuade the Russians to leave the area and rejoin the American Army farther on. They could speak some French and English, but they acted as if they didn't know what we were saying.

We then sought help from our nearest Army headquarters. A detachment of military policemen was assigned to put the Russians on a train bound for an Army headquarters in Rennes. We were very relieved when the train pulled out of the station in our area, but we learned later that when the train stopped at a station 50 miles away, the Russians got off and disappeared. That was far out of our civil affairs area, so we had no further dealings with the Russian renegades.

Our D2G1 detachment had moved with the 29th Division all the way across Brittany to the Brest area in the last week of August of 1944. The U.S. Army and our allies, the British and Canadians, were in desperate need of a major port, such as Brest, since our personnel, supplies and equipment still were being brought in over the beaches in Normandy.

Brest was a major German submarine base of operations, and the city and port were heavily defended by veteran German troops, including one hardened parachute division. During a siege of several weeks, the Germans each day set a long row of houses and buildings on fire as their defense line against our attacking forces. Thousands of lives were lost, and much of the city of Brest was destroyed.

Ironically, by the time the siege ended in late September, the Brest port was no longer needed, inasmuch as other ports at Le Havre and Antwerp had been captured by the Allies.

In the Brest area, the first destination of our D2G1 detachment was the quaint village of Ploudalmezeau. We were told later by French friends that as we came into the north part of Ploudalmezeau, the Germans were leaving the south part.

At Ploudalmezeau, our detachment assisted another civil affairs detachment in handling refugee problems. Thousands of people had fled to the small towns to the north of Brest, leaving in such haste before the battle began that they had brought no provisions.

Our civil affairs detachments assisted mayors of the various cantons in setting up free food canteens, establishing refugee camps and giving other aid to the refugees who had doubled and tripled the populations of what had been small communities.

We were instrumental in getting medical supplies to distressed people on the Island of Ouessant, off the tip of Brittany. French fishermen slipped these supplies to the island in small fishing boats under the noses of the Germans, who still occupied the island.

Our detachment also gave whatever aid we could to French Resistance troops, who were clearing the area of German stragglers.

First aid treatment for the refugees was given by two French public health nurses, Madame LeGuen and Mademoiselle Gold, who were attached to our D2G1 detachment.

In Ploudalmezeau, I became well acquainted with a wonderful French family named Jaouën. Both of the parents were chemists and operated the town's pharmacy. Over the years Ruth and I have become very close to two Jaouën sisters, Anne-Yvonne and Marie-Thérèse Bleünven. In mid-September during the Battle of Brest, we moved to another small town, St. Renan, which was the headquarters of a canton immediately to the north of Brest. In St. Renan I stayed in the home of the Cheminant family, who were closely related to the Jaouëns in Ploudalmezeau.

Our detachment area included three adjoining cantons, and much of our work was still related to the problems of refugees, of whom there were more than 20,000 in our area.

We also often received special assignments. At St. Renan, for example, we obtained the services of a French marine unit for de-mining fortified areas along the seacoast.

Another special assignment involved horses, which had become the property of the U.S. Army after the battle of Brest. The Germans were supposed to have had a very modern army, but they still had a lot of horse-drawn equipment.

When the battle at Brest ended, the U.S. Army technically became the owner of a large number of horses that had been brought into that part of France by the Germans. As temporary caretakers of the horses, the mayors at the canton headquarters had registered all the horses with numbers chiseled on their hooves and then turned the horses over to farmers who needed them in their farming.

Without any explanation, our nearest Army headquarters in Rennes sent us an order for 30 horses. We were ordered to have 10 horses ready for a pickup on three Saturday mornings two weeks apart at a nearby town named Plugerneau.

For the first delivery, Major Viault asked me to contact the mayors of 10 cantons early in the week and have them each deliver one horse on Saturday morning to Plugerneau. On that first Saturday morning, 10 fine, healthy horses were ready for pickup by trucks from the Army headquarters at Rennes.

Since our next horse delivery was not due for two weeks, Major Viault said he wanted to make the long trip to Rennes and spend several days there. For the second pickup of 10 horses he took it upon himself to contact the 10 mayors for the second delivery of horses.

Then when I went to Plugerneau for the second Saturday pickup, the scene was unbelievable. There were 10 horses all right, but skinny old horses that could hardly stand up. They weren't even fit for a glue factory. The soldiers driving the trucks were just shaking their heads as they loaded the horses and drove off toward Rennes.

Knowing Major Viault's strong sympathy for the French, I realized that he knew something I didn't know.

"What really happened?" I asked.

He replied: "We've got to make sure that no one else knows. I couldn't figure out why our Army suddenly wanted horses because we don't have any horse-drawn equipment.

"When I made that trip to Rennes, I spent an evening at the officers' club, where usually you can find out what really is going on. I learned that the only reason the Army headquarters wanted horses was to set up a riding stable for the officers.

"I felt that it was far more important for the French farmers to have those horses because they needed them so badly, far more than some Army officers wanting to set up a private riding stable.

"So, when I contacted the mayors of those 10 cantons, I suggested that they might want to give us some of the worst horses they could find, and all of them got the message."

A few days later we received a message from the Rennes headquarters canceling the horse order.

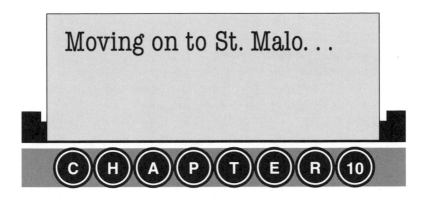

Moving on to St. Malo. . .

C H A P T E R 10

In mid-November, our detachment moved from the Brest area to St. Malo, another picturesque part of coastal Brittany. St. Malo is an ancient walled city with a small port which once was used by the French corsairs preying on British ships. Adjoining St. Malo were two other cities, St. Servan and Paramé.

Lying across a bay of the Rance River is a popular resort city, Dinard. When we were there, St. Malo and Dinard were linked across the bay by a ferry, a small motor boat.

A short distance offshore from St. Malo is a fairly good-sized island which can be reached by foot over the sand at low tide. As a defense measure, the Germans had fortified the island with large artillery guns and had poured concrete for underground quarters for the soldiers.

In fierce resistance to the American Army, the Germans had destroyed most of St. Malo, leaving only a few buildings intact.

As a few Americans had done before us, Major Viault and I moved into the Hotel Univers, one of the buildings not damaged. We had our civil affairs office in a more central location in the adjacent city of St. Servan.

Late one morning we were visited by the madam of the House of Joy in Dinard and two of her young ladies. They had come from Dinard in the motor boat ferry.

She reported that her establishment had been visited the night before by American sailors from a small boat that had been anchored in the bay.

"They seemed like a very nice group of young men," she said, "but after they had gone, I discovered that all my money and my good purse were missing."

Major Viault said, "We want to help you by making a thorough investigation. Lieutenant Buck here is a former Chicago newspaperman who also knows a lot about police work. He can start the investigation right away by going back with you and looking around your place and asking all the necessary questions."

So off I went with the madam to Dinard.

The upshot of it all was that I found the madam's purse in the yard where it apparently had been tossed by one of the departing American sailors.

"This is great," I told her. "We can get the fingerprints off this purse and then probably find out who the sailor was. The Army has a criminal investigation unit in Rennes, and I will send the purse there to see what fingerprints they can find. This should probably take a week or two."

I returned on the ferry to St. Malo with the madam's purse.

I sent the purse by a special messenger to an Army criminal investigation unit in Rennes, but as time went by it became more and more embarrassing. Apparently, the purse had been lost, and we kept reassuring the madam who was complaining that everything was being done to find it.

The whereabouts of the madam's purse was still unknown when our D2G1 detachment moved on. Six months later, I was having lunch at an officers' club in Le Mans when two officers of a criminal investigation unit sat down across from me. They obviously were upset about something, and they seemed to just want to tell anyone who would listen about it.

"We have to go all the way to St. Malo just to settle a case," one of them explained. "This complaint came to the attention of General Eisenhower's headquarters, and we were ordered to investigate and make an immediate settlement.

"It is hard to believe, but all that this involves is a purse that was owned by the madam of a brothel in Dinard. Some goofy lieutenant who thought he was a detective took the purse to get fingerprints when he was investigating the robbing of the madam's brothel by a bunch of sailors one night. The purse was lost and the madam has been pestering the Eisenhower headquarters with letters asking for a settlement. We have been ordered to make a settlement with the madam so she will stop complaining."

Needless to say, I listened without saying anything.

In December of 1955, the editor of the *Chicago Tribune* asked those of us who had been overseas during World War II to write about a Christmas that had a special meaning for us. I wrote about the Christmas in 1944 when our D2G1 detachment was in St. Malo. My strory about the German breakthrough in the Belgian Ardennes read:

> We were hundreds of miles from the fighting, but we were nonetheless worried about the welfare of our Army. Major Viault and I felt a special need for attending a church service. Although neither of us was Catholic, we accompanied two French friends to midnight Mass in the cathedral.
>
> Our French friends—one a provincial correspondent for a Paris newspaper and the other the curator of the local museum—were as worried as we were. They feared that the newly won liberation of France might soon be lost.
>
> As we approached the cathedral, I made known a personal fear. It concerned my brother, Ralph, who was a lieutenant in charge of an advanced artillery observation detachment.
>
> His last letter had been written several days before a German attack, which occurred nine days before

Christmas. The German army had smashed through American defenses with a surprise attack in the Belgian Ardennes, and all reports had indicated that the American and Allied armies were being disastrously overrun.

After the midnight Mass, our French friends invited us to join them and their families at an early Christmas morning dinner, an old Yuletide custom in the French hinterlands. Then, late on Christmas day, we were the hosts to our French friends at a typical American holiday dinner of turkey, supplied by the Army Quartermaster Corps.

As our dinner party was breaking up, each of our two French friends drew me aside. Separately, they told me the same thing.

"At midnight Mass, we said many, many special prayers," they said. "And one of those special prayers was that your brother was safe and would be all right."

Later, I was to learn that my brother had been ordered to pull his detachment off the front lines six hours before the German attack. He escaped unharmed after his battalion had been surrounded for three days in what was to become the Battle of the Bulge.

In St. Malo we became acquainted with a most unusual husband and wife who, as French Resistance leaders, achieved remarkable feats of courage during the German occupation of France.

Roger and Aimee Pansart became lifelong friends.

They operated a popular tourist bus service along the Brittany coast between St. Malo and the famous Mont St. Michel. They had homes in Paramé and on a nearby farm, where the house and farm buildings were enclosed by a high wall.

As French Resistance leaders, they specialized in saving the crews of American and other Allied bombers who had been shot down by the Germans. The high wall at the Pansart farm home helped to provide a safe haven for the

Allied airmen until they could be shipped safely to England in small fishing boats.

Madame Pansart recalled that one American pilot liked his visit in France so much that he stayed for 30 days and finally had to be persuaded to take a fishing boat back to England.

"He seemed to be a real daredevil," said Madame Pansart. "He was fluent in French, and he borrowed some of my husband's clothes to go to St. Malo as a civilian. If the Germans had caught him, they would have killed him as a spy."

During the German occupation, French civilians had little or no gasoline for their automobiles and trucks. As a result, some French drivers rigged up steam-operated equipment for their vehicles. This special steam-operated equipment included a small boiler heated by wood on a small grate.

Monsieur Pansart had such steam-operated equipment on the truck he used to pick up the American and Allied airmen after they had parachuted.

"We had something of a crisis one time when I ran out of water in the boiler," recalled Monsieur Pansart. "One night a friend of mine and I had picked up two American pilots, whom we hid in the back of the truck under straw. We were almost home, probably a kilometer or so away, when we ran out of water and steam.

"Fortunately, none of us had relieved ourselves for quite a while. So, how do you suppose that two Frenchmen and two American pilots were able to get the truck going again to make it all the way home?"

My wife, Ruth, met the Pansarts when we visited St. Malo during our honeymoon in June of 1953.

Ruth surely must have been taken back a bit at first. As we were crossing the square in St. Malo, Madame Pansart suddenly came running up shouting, "Lieutenant Buck! Lieutenant Buck!"

She flung her arms around me and began kissing me on the cheeks. Ruth never said so, but I have often wondered if she might not have been thinking, "This must be one of my new husband's old French girlfriends he didn't tell me about."

In September 1969, Madame Pansart helped to plan a celebration of the 25th anniversary of the liberation of St. Malo by the American Army. At Madame Pansart's invitation, Ruth and I, daughter Mary and son Tom, with French friends from Paris, arranged to be there for the celebration.

Arriving the evening before the event, I was surprised and dumbfounded when Madame Pansart informed me that I was to have a major role in the event.

"You are to be introduced as Captain John T. Buck, the American savior of St. Malo," explained Madame Pansart.

I was almost lost for words.

"Madame Pansart, you can't say that," I said. "I didn't get to St. Malo until two months after the battle was over."

She replied, "Nobody will know the difference. You have to do this for us because we need you. We have a political situation here that has caused the American embassy in Paris to decline to send us an official representative for our celebration."

I agreed to go along with the act after she said that the celebration would not have any real meaning without an American soldier taking part.

During the anniversary morning, I represented the United States by laying wreaths at war memorial monuments in Paramé, St. Servan, and Dinard. Then came the big celebration at noon in the square at St. Malo, where more than 5,000 people were present. I received a further surprise when, as part of my introduction to the assemblage, I was identified not only as the savior of St. Malo but also as a special envoy of President Nixon.

My brief remarks in English brought a loud burst of applause.

As the ceremony was ending, I noticed an American colonel in uniform in the audience. We were invited to a civic luncheon in the nearby museum, and as we were entering, the American colonel came up to me and asked, "Who are you?"

"You heard the introduction about my being a special envoy of President Nixon, didn't you?" I replied.

After the luncheon, which lasted more than two hours, there was only a brief intermission before we gathered again in the walled garden of the mayor of St. Malo for an official reception. While there, I felt that I had to tell the colonel, who was still present, who I really was.

The colonel's response was a warm-hearted chuckle.

Later, we learned that Madame Pansart had received the American Freedom Medal, the highest award to a civilian, from President Eisenhower, the commander of the Allied forces in World War II.

After serving two months in St. Malo we moved on for relatively short assignments in Orleans, Chartres and then ended our tour of duty in Le Mans. We also made weekly trips to Blois and Tours.

As the war ended in Europe, General Eisenhower's SHAEF headquarters believed that something should be done to keep soldiers occupied in a positive way while waiting to have enough points for going home. It was decided to have the various army units provide educational programs with junior officers serving as teachers. To train the junior officers, the Army set up a school at the City University in Paris for a one-week course.

As a first lieutenant, I was assigned to take the course in Paris and then return to my civil affairs detachment in Le Mans to teach our GIs.

It was a great week in Paris. We stayed in a comfortable dormitory on the City University campus, spent five hours a day in the classroom, and had the late afternoon and evening free for anything we wanted to do.

One of our best lecturers was the actress Madeleine Carroll, who as a volunteer was serving with the American Red Cross in Europe. For her lectures, it was standing-room-only in the classroom.

Her subject was the relationship between American soldiers and French civilians. For one thing, she explained that there was a need to do something about the crudeness of some soldiers who seemed to think of French women as ladies of the night, interested only in sex.

"Just the other day I had an experience myself about this," she said.

"I was walking along the Champs-Elysees when all of a sudden I felt a tap on my shoulder.

"Turning around, I found myself face to face with a tall, gawky GI.

"His eyes seemed to pop out as he blurted:

" 'My god! Madeleine Carroll! You, too?'

"Then he turned and ran off as fast as he could."

For her work with the Red Cross, Madeleine Carroll received France's Legion of Honor and the U.S. Medal of Freedom. She was a highly educated and lovely lady of the stage and screen who made 40 films.

In early August, after the European war had ended, our D2G1 civil affairs detachment was disbanded, and each of us was given an individual assignment for the rest of our time in Europe. I was assigned to the SHAEF headquarters in Frankfurt, Germany.

It sounds absurd, but I worked in a special office with the job of keeping track of German officials who had recanted and denounced their Nazi beliefs. In fact, we had a running total of the number of Germans who had been politically born-again.

During this period "going home" was based on the number of points one had earned for time and service, time overseas, number of combat zones and other important types of service.

Day-by-day departure of homebound soldiers caused our office staff to be in such a flux that the list of people on duty was taken every morning.

This provided the real highlight of my service in that office as I was able to fulfill a promise I had been making for the last year and a half.

While overseas, I received a letter about once every six months from my former English teacher at Indiana University, Miss Edna Johnson. Miss Johnson had a brother who was a journalist and was such a close friend of a well-known cartoonist, Gaar Williams, that he had named a son after him.

In each of her letters Miss Johnson asked me to look up her nephew, Gaar Williams Johnson, who, she said, was a private first class in Europe. I had promised to do so, even though I knew that would be almost impossible since there were well over 3 million American soldiers in Europe at that time.

One morning, in making a check of who was in the office that day, a private first class handed me a pad on which I was to write my name showing my presence. Above the space for my signature was the name "PFC Gaar Williams Johnson."

"Who in the world is this Gaar Williams Johnson?" I asked.

"I am Gaar Williams Johnson," replied the PFC with the check-in pad.

I immediately wrote a letter to Miss Johnson pointing out that I always tried to keep my promises and that I had finally met her nephew.

Not long afterwards my points for going home came due, and I began my journey home which included three weeks on a Liberty Ship that first ran aground in the English Channel. After being moved to Southampton our ship was inspected and declared seaworthy for its crossing to New York City.

In June of 1984 I had the pleasure of being with a group of former war correspondents, soldiers and two Red Cross "girls," (as we called them during the war) who were celebrating the 40th anniversary of the D-Day invasion of Normandy. Altogether there were 38 of us.

For 10 days we rode in a bus across southern England and then in Normandy for the various ceremonies that took place. Between stops, everyone took turns at a microphone to recall his or her wartime experiences, which involved either D-Day or arrival in Normandy shortly thereafter.

As people told their stories, I held a small tape recorder against a speaker next to my seat. I really did this without thinking, but after I got home I realized I had some very interesting oral history. I added introductions to each of the speakers, along with music from World War II to produce four tapes totaling six hours.

One of the first places we visited was a small but very significant museum in a building near Southampton, known as Southwick House, which had housed the Supreme Headquarters for the invasion. The significance of Southwick House is told in a plaque that reads:

"In this room, at 0415 (4:15 a.m.) on the 5th day of June of 1944 General Dwight D. Eisenhower, the Supreme Allied Commander, made the historic decision to launch the assault against the continent of Europe on the sixth day of June despite uncertain weather conditions."

A member of our group, Barney Oldfield, a Los Angeles public relations man, provided details about the critical decision that General Eisenhower had made.

Oldfield, an American paratrooper with the rank of colonel, had had a very unusual assignment. He was one of three officers who had the special duty of issuing communiqués for Field Marshal Montgomery, the top British commander. The other two of the trio were British and Canadian officers.

Oldfield said that shortly after the invasion a correspondent for *Reader's Digest* obtained an exclusive footnote about Eisenhower's decision; but for some reason or another, it was never published.

"The *Reader's Digest* correspondent wanted to get an interview with Eisenhower," explained Oldfield. "But General Eisenhower was not available, so we arranged for the correspondent to interview someone else."

The interview was with Vice-Admiral Sir Bertram Ramsay, who, as commander of the Navy for the invasion, was one of several top commanders present when Eisenhower made the decision.

The correspondent wanted to know what General Eisenhower actually said when he made the decision.

Admiral Ramsay had given a good summary of the meeting, but he looked somewhat puzzled when asked about Eisenhower's actual words in making the decision. The admiral explained that it was "some kind of a quaint American expression" about which he was not exactly sure. He "pondered a little bit," looked out of the window and then said:

"It was kind of a Kansas expression. Do you have a term in America that sounds like 'Let her rip'?"

Oldfield said the *Reader's Digest* correspondent replied, "We sure do."

Oldfield said American history books should be revised because they say that Eisenhower said, "Well, we'll go."

"The expression 'Let her rip,' must be correct," said Oldfield, "because it sounds like Eisenhower."

In another of his recollections, Oldfield said that it took an old-fashioned way to get the first press dispatch from Normandy to England on D-Day—that is, the first written, hard copy dispatch. By the "old-fashioned way," I mean the homing or carrier pigeon.

Oldfield said he was in General Montgomery's office in London on the evening of D-Day when word was received that a carrier pigeon had been found at Dover, the port city on the English Channel.

Strapped to the pigeon's leg was a capsule with a piece of tissue that read:

"Normandy—landed with 101st." Signed, "Rubin, Reuters."

Oldfield said it was "unbelievable."

"Here we had a communication system for the invasion forces that could handle an estimated 100 million words in a 24-hour period. But the first printed word from Normandy came by way of a pigeon."

Oldfield explained that the Reuters correspondent, Robert Rubin, had taken two homing pigeons with him when he jumped with the 101st Airborne division in Normandy. Each pigeon had a capsule with the short message of Rubin's landing.

"He held the pigeons down in his hands to keep them from being ripped away in the propeller blasts of the airplanes and then released them as he landed."

That was late on the night of June 5th, when the paratroopers invaded Normandy. The pigeon with the message was found at 9 o'clock on the evening of June 6th.

I could have said, "Gee, we were using carrier pigeons five years earlier in Chicago journalism."

My Years with
the <u>Tribune</u>

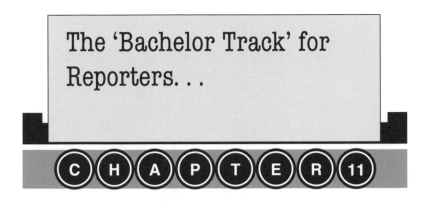

The 'Bachelor Track' for Reporters. . .

CHAPTER 11

In December 1945, I returned to Chicago and the *Tribune* where I had been promised a job. Early in World War II, Colonel McCormick announced that all *Tribune* employees going off to war could have their jobs back when the war was over.

If I had really been interested in my first assignment at the *Tribune*, I might have become another Warren Buffett, a man of great investment wealth. For nine months before the war and about a year and a half afterwards, I was assigned to the Financial News Department. While I found financial news somewhat interesting, I really wasn't obsessed with it; so I missed a chance of becoming wealthy through the wise purchases of stocks and bonds.

In 1947, I was transferred to the City staff, first as a swing rewrite man and then as a local government reporter. For many of my years at the *Tribune*, I worked the best of hours—from 10 A.M. to 5 P.M. on weekdays— although there was little or no time for lunch. After a morning usually in the County Building or City Hall, I came to the office at noon to write any stories I already had, and then I went out again in the afternoon for other stories to be written by a 5 o'clock deadline.

I had such a variety of local government news sources that I always had at least one significant news story every day and sometimes several. As a regular beat, I covered the Cook County Building, which included the Cook County Board of Commissioners, the Sheriff's Office, the County Clerk, the County Treasurer, the Assessor, the Recorder and the civil branch of the States Attorney's Office.

In addition, I was the regular reporter covering the Chicago Transit Authority, operator of the bus and elevated-subway systems, the City Plan Commission, and the Slum Clearance Board. Another busy part of my regular beat was the Chicago Housing Authority, builder and operator of public housing for low-income tenants.

As an offshoot of my city planning assignment, I also covered the monthly meetings of the Board of Trustees of the University of Illinois, initially in relation to the U. of I. plans for and construction of its Chicago campus.

In the first eight years following World War II, I was a bachelor, and as a result I was given assignments that were considered appropriate only for bachelors. These assignments pertained to the investigation of vice—striptease joints, brothels and sleazy nightclubs.

Tourism and conventions were big business in Chicago, and the city fathers often became concerned about reports that visiting businessmen were in danger of being doped and robbed in questionable places. One businessman from a North Shore suburb of Chicago had been last seen in a striptease joint and never heard of again.

I was assigned to spend several nights on the town posing as a visiting businessman to do a series of five articles. For my protection, the *Tribune* arranged for the police commissioner, Timothy O'Connor, to assign two young plainclothes detectives to accompany me.

Besides observing questionable activities in the striptease taverns and the lower class nightclubs, we also discovered several large brothels and gambling joints. Commissioner O'Connor said he would have to order immediate raids on the places because it would be improper for him to allow them to continue operation when he had full knowledge of the situation.

If the commissioner were to order immediate raids, however, my series of five articles would have been pointless. I planned to use the large brothels and gambling joints as examples in the leads for five different stories. Commissioner O'Connor reluctantly agreed to hold off the raids until the places had been mentioned in my *Tribune* articles.

It worked this way. My articles about vice did not appear until the first final edition came out at midnight, rather than appearing in the early evening editions. At Commissioner O'Connor's instruction, a special squad was standing by to see which place was mentioned in the article so that a raid could then be made immediately.

As a footnote to that investigation, I should mention that one of the young detectives helping me later married the madam of one of the brothels we discovered. After the marriage, however, the bride completely changed her way of life and became a normal homemaker.

With the help of the deputy sheriff, I also did a series of articles on vice and other illegal operations in suburban areas of Cook County. One of the main results of that investigation was a crackdown by the sheriff and suburban police departments against slot machines, which were in widespread illegal use throughout the county.

One weekend I collaborated with another *Tribune* reporter, Clay Gowran, in an investigation of vice in downstate Kankakee and in Kankakee County. Brothels were reported to be operating without any interference by local law officials, luring many customers from Chicago and Cook County.

It was a rewarding experience to work with Clay Gowran, who was a top-notch writer and reporter. He also

The **Chicago Tribune** newsroom in 1948 was a hubbub of noise and interaction, as this "keyed" photo shows. Among those in the newsroom were: (1) J. Loy Maloney, managing editor; (2) Don Maxwell, city editor; (3) Stewart Owen, news editor; (4) Wallace Abbey, makeup editor; (5) Eleanor Page, society editor; (6) Anne Douglas Bayless, reporter; (7) Herschel Patterson, a financial news editor; (8) Tom Buck, reporter, talking with (9) Ora Willis, "slot man," i.e., chief of the local news copy-editing desk.

was known for his ingenuity in carrying out difficult assignments. He died unexpectedly at an early age, and the *Tribune* ran a feature story about him with this headline: "One of the Very Good Ones."

Our Kankakee weekend assignment was to observe the vice activities on Saturday night and then early Sunday write a detailed story for the front page in the Monday morning *Tribune*. News often was pretty scarce on Sundays, so a special effort was made to get interesting stories for the Monday morning edition.

Gowran and I found the vice operations to be concentrated in two large brothels in the city of Kankakee (one near the railroad station) and a third brothel on a major highway about 10 miles east of the city.

The brothel on the highway was housed in a large T-shaped wooden building on the edge of a cornfield. At the front of the building was a bar room from which two doors led into another spacious section filled with slot machines. The prostitutes, who had rooms in a long, motel-type section toward the rear, approached their customers as they were playing the slot machines.

We were staying at the Kankakee Hotel, and during a late breakfast on Sunday morning we went over our notes. At noon, Gowran got the *Tribune* on the line and began dictating our story.

He had almost finished a long story on our observations of the Saturday night activities when he was told by an assistant editor that a change in strategy had been ordered. He said that Don Maxwell, then the city editor, had seen Gowran's copy and thought it was very good, but that a different approach should be taken.

"As everyone knows, the *Tribune* is a Republican newspaper," said the assistant editor. "Instead of embarrassing the Republicans with a story like this, we should make them look good. The assignment now is to have the authorities raid all these places this afternoon or early evening and get a special session of the court this evening to have the madams and the prostitutes fined. That would show that the Republicans are cleaning up Kankakee County."

This was where Gowran's ingenuity saved the day for us. At first, it appeared that the arrest and a Sunday evening court session would be impossible.

We telephoned three key officials in Kankakee—the mayor, the sheriff and the prosecuting attorney. After introducing ourselves and telling them what we had found on Saturday evening, we explained that the *Tribune* would like to have them, as good Republicans, help us with the assignment by having the brothels raided and the women arrested and found guilty at a Sunday evening session of court.

Before abruptly hanging up, the mayor said, "Are you kidding?"

We got similar replies from the sheriff and the prosecuting attorney, each of whom hung up on us.

I recall Clay's saying, "There must be an association of ministers. We could keep this controversy stirred up if we could get some of the ministers to go along with us for a tour of the brothels."

We were able to get the president of the ministerial association on the telephone. Without any hesitation he said that he and some of his fellow ministers would be glad to make the tour of the brothels, but that they couldn't do it until after their early Sunday evening services.

In less than an hour, however, their plan to visit the brothels apparently was leaked to the three public officials whom we had contacted earlier. We received calls from each of them.

"When do you want these raids made?" asked the mayor.

"When do you want that brothel east of town raided?" asked the sheriff.

"What time do you want the court session?" asked the state's attorney.

To make sure that the raids were made, Gowran went with the city police on one of the Kankakee raids, and I went with the sheriff in raiding the brothel on the highway east of the city.

As we entered the highway brothel, a man had hit the jackpot on one of the slot machines in the room behind the bar. He seemed to panic, apparently not knowing whether to pick up the money or not.

"Pick up your money and get out of here," ordered a deputy sheriff. "We're only interested in the women, not the customers."

I was still with the raiding squad when they returned to the sheriff's office. One of the deputies asked, "Who should sign these arrest warrants?"

The sheriff replied, "The damn *Chicago Tribune* should have signed them."

Altogether, three madams and 12 ladies of the night appeared before the judge, and all were fined. The fines were promptly paid, and they all went on their way.

The top eight-column headline on the front page of the Monday morning *Chicago Tribune* read: "Republicans Clean Up Kankakee County."

On Wednesday, two days later, we received a phone call from the president of the ministerial association in Kankakee.

"Please come back," said the minister. "All those places are going wide open again."

We told our editor, Don Maxwell, about the call.

"No, " said Maxwell. "I think we've had enough of this. Let's forget it."

In newspaper reporting, it sometimes seems unbelievable how one thing can lead to another—how a series of otherwise unrelated things can be tied together in a meaningful way.

As a bachelor in 1949, I was assigned to a swing shift, filling in for other staff members on their days off. Two nights a week I substituted as a rewrite man from 9 o'clock at night to 6 o'clock the next morning. Working for a night editor, I handled only major stories for which the front page was changed in what was called a "replate." With the very latest news, these replated editions were sold at early morning news stands, mostly in the downtown area.

In 1949, the *Tribune* was experiencing the last part of a 22-month strike by the printers' union. Because of the strike, the *Tribune* had developed an effective but difficult and sometimes time-consuming process for printing the paper and making changes with replates.

It was about 4 o'clock on a June morning when we received a report that two 12-year-old boys from a South Side military academy were believed to have been kidnapped. One of the boys was a son of James McCarthy, manager of a Near North Side nightclub, the Club Alabam.

The owner of the Club Alabam, which was located on Rush Street a half-block south of Chicago Avenue, was said to be resisting a move by gangsters to take over the club. It was feared that gangsters had kidnapped the boys.

After writing a short front-page story about the reported kidnapping, I was finished for the night and left to have breakfast.

At Rush and Ohio Street, I was about to enter the Corner House restaurant when I noticed two boys in military uniforms walking south toward me on Rush Street. When they reached me, I introduced myself and invited them in to have breakfast. They told me that they had planned to visit the Club Alabam, where one boy's father worked, but they had gotten cold feet and instead slept for an hour or two in a vacant lot next to the nightclub. They said they had intended to walk back to the academy on the South Side.

After we had ordered breakfast, I went to the telephone and called the night editor, Bob Johnson, to tell him that I had found the boys and would bring them in as soon as we finished breakfast.

Somewhat amazed by what had happened, Bob Johnson said he would call the police and the Club Alabam.

As a result of this incident, I became well acquainted with Jimmy McCarthy and his staff at the Club Alabam. During that summer of 1949, several friends and I, after working late at the *Tribune*, would drop by the Club Alabam for a late-night beer.

We became acquainted with an attractive singer and comedienne, Jeanne Kerin, and had fun providing her with jokes—some of which she could use.

That fall, the Club Alabam became a thing of the past for me after I was assigned to a daytime beat covering the Cook County Building and other local governmental offices.

About a year and a half later, on a late afternoon in February, I was writing a dull real estate tax story in the *Tribune* City Room when our managing editor, J. Loy Maloney, called me over to his desk.

"Please see Frank Winge about finding the body of Ralph Capone, Jr. and doing a story on him," said Maloney.

I was quite baffled and said, "I'm sorry, but I don't know anything about Capone."

Maloney said, "Winge tells me that you're the only one who can find the body of Ralph Capone, Jr., so see him about it."

Frank Winge, who had been an outstanding police reporter during the "Front Page" era, was the night assignment editor and was known to have been acquainted with almost everyone in Chicago, from gangsters all the way up to people in high society.

"I'm sure you have never forgotten that attractive singer and comedienne some of you fellows used to see in the Club Alabam," said Winge. "We have a report that Ralph Capone, Jr. has died, but the family does not want to have any publicity, and no one will say where the body is. That comedienne you used to know at the Club Alabam was a girlfriend of Capone, Jr.; and I have an idea that if you can find her, you can find out where the body is and can get a story about his death."

It was then about 5 P.M., and the first thing I did was to call Jimmy McCarthy at the Club Alabam and ask if he knew where Jeanne Kerin was. McCarthy said he didn't know, but he would try to find out and call me back.

A half-hour later McCarthy called and said that they could not find exactly where she was but that she was believed to be performing somewhere in the Minneapolis area.

At that time, the *Tribune* had a large staff of telephone operators; so I called the chief telephone operator, explained our problem, and asked if she and her staff could canvass various nightclubs in the Minneapolis area to try to locate Jeanne Kerin.

It was almost 7 o'clock when our chief telephone operator called and told me where there had found Jeanne Kerin, and gave me the telephone number where she was performing.

I called immediately and got her on the line.

"I'll tell you, Tom, because I think you will understand and do the right story," said Jeanne, as she tried to hold back her sobbing. "Ralph and I have been in love for a long while, but it couldn't continue. He had a family, and it was just wrong for us to go on as we had. So I decided the only way was to break it off. For the last week, he had been calling me from a hotel room in Chicago where he obviously was drinking. It's awful, but I think he just drank himself to death."

In my story for the *Tribune*, I wrote that Ralph Capone, Jr. had committed suicide by drinking himself to death because of an unrequited love. Later, Jeanne Kerin received a note he had left her.

His note read: "I love you. I love you. Jeannie, only you I love. Only you. I'm gone."

A medical report showed that Capone had been mixing Scotch with pills.

Incidentally, Ralph Capone, Jr. had not been using his real name. He had been using the name of Ralph Gabriele—Gabriele having been the first name of his Capone grandfather.

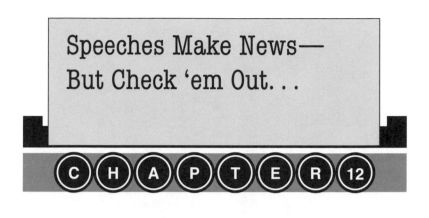

Speeches Make News—
But Check 'em Out. . .

C H A P T E R 12

With so many conventions and public events taking place in Chicago, newspaper editors for many years considered speeches to be important news.

As a reporter for the *Tribune* in downtown Chicago, I covered hundreds of talks and speeches. Because I was usually readily available in the County Building or City Hall, I often got last-minute assignments to cover luncheon speeches.

It is normal practice for public relations representatives of companies and organizations to provide texts of speeches in advance of the presentations. Besides being available at the conventions, the advance copies were often sent directly to the newspapers.

The best structure of a speech was said to consist of three parts. First, the speaker should say what he was going to tell them. Then he should tell them. Then he should say what he had just told them.

Since many speeches were written in this pattern, it was very easy to evaluate advance copies quickly simply by reading the conclusions on the last page. If a story was written solely from an advance copy, however, it was critical to make certain that the speaker actually gave the speech.

At work in the Chicago Tribune *newsroom were colleagues Pulitzer Prize-winning reporter George Bliss (right) and Tom Buck.*

As a financial news reporter for the *Tribune*, I was once asked by the assistant financial editor, Phil Hampson, to drop by the Palmer House during the latter part of the noon hour to check on a speaker at a drug manufacturers' convention.

"We plan to do a story from the advance copy, but we want to be sure that the speaker is there and delivers it," said Hampson. "Just give us a ring after you have been there and made sure that the speech was given."

As I walked into the convention dining room at the Palmer House, people were standing up, and there seemed to be a lot of tension.

"Is there something special going on here?" I asked a man near the entrance.

"There sure is," he replied. "Our speaker just dropped dead as he was starting his speech."

Just then, two men (apparently paramedics) came through the crowd carrying a stretcher with a body on it. Without hesitating, I fell in behind them and followed them as they went to a nearby elevator.

No one asked me who I was as I got into the elevator, rode up several floors, got off and went with them into a room where the man's family was staying.

Without being asked for identification, I stood in the room listening for 15 or 20 minutes as a policeman, a deputy coroner, a doctor and a representative of the hotel talked with the widow and the family and made necessary arrangements. After all of the others had left the room, I identified myself to the widow and her family and asked if they would give me information for an obituary in the *Tribune*.

The widow and other family members were very cooperative in giving information about the deceased, who was president of one of the country's largest pharmaceutical companies.

Quite by coincidence, in leaving, I took an elevator on which the hotel's public relations man and his assistant were riding. I recognized the public relations man, but he didn't know me.

"This is a good example of how we handle a death," the public relations man told his assistant. "It is never very good public relations to have anyone dying in a hotel. As far as the public is concerned, no one ever dies in a hotel.

"It doesn't make much difference to fudge a little by reporting that a hotel death took place somewhere else. In the case today, I have already called the City News Bureau and told them this man died on the sidewalk on State Street, in front of the Palmer House."

As we were getting off the elevator in the lobby, I couldn't resist the opportunity to identify myself to the Palmer House public relations man.

"I am a *Tribune* reporter who worked for the City News Bureau not long ago," I said, "and the first thing I'm going to do now is call City News and tell them the truth—about how you have lied to them about where this man died."

I walked to the nearby pay telephones, leaving the public relations man with his mouth open.

I made the first call to my former City News mentor, Larry Mulay, the city editor; then I called Phil Hampson at the *Tribune* to tell him about the death of the speaker. Hampson said he would kill the story about the speech, and suggested that I call the *Tribune's* City Desk to turn in the information for an obituary.

The next day I received a telephone call from a friend, Ed Spear, who was a financial news reporter for the *Chicago Sun-Times*. At that time, the early editions of the morning newspapers—the *Tribune* and the *Sun-Times*— were on the news stands as early as 5 o'clock the evening before.

Ed told me that he had almost been fired because he had written a story on the drug manufacturer's talk from the advanced copy without checking to see if he had delivered it.

"I was reading my story and admiring it in the early edition on my way home last evening on the Elston Avenue streetcar," Ed said. "I also had picked up an early edition of the *Tribune*. When I turned to the *Tribune* and read the obituary about the man who had supposedly given the speech, I almost broke a leg jumping off the streetcar to get to the telephone to tell my office what had happened and that my story on the speech should be killed."

Years later, as a teacher of journalism at Loyola University, Chicago, I cited this story as an example of how journalists should always double-check everything.

It also was a good example of how one could be present as an uninvited observer merely by keeping quiet and acting as if one belonged there.

Of all the speakers I covered for the *Tribune*, there are only a few who were memorable.

One was Adlai Stevenson, the Illinois governor and later Democratic presidential candidate, who was among the very best speakers I ever heard. Unlike most speakers, who had ghostwriters, Stevenson wrote most of his own speeches, and they were classics. Not only were they well written, they sparkled with humor. Samples should be included in every speechwriting textbook.

In 1965, Stevenson was the principal speaker at a ceremony celebrating a Lake Michigan landfill addition to the Evanston campus of Northwestern University. It was an outdoor ceremony, and a speaker's platform had been set up on the top of a very low, one-story building at the edge of the landfill. It was a sunny mild day but extremely windy.

Stevenson was about halfway through his talk when a strong gust of wind blew away several pages of his text.

"From now on, no one can ever say that an ill wind doesn't blow some good," quipped Stevenson.

Another excellent political speaker was former Governor Harold Handley of Indiana, who spoke occasionally at Chicago civic lunches. His speeches were unusual in that they consisted mostly of modern parables which aptly illustrated the points he was making.

I never will forget a speech given shortly after World War II by Senator C. Wayland Brooks of Illinois, who began with this story to emphasize the grave danger of atom bombs:

"Atomic war broke out throughout the world to the extent that only one spot in a jungle was left untouched," said Senator Brooks. "After the smoke had cleared, a pair of baboons came out of the jungle and stood looking around with amazement.

"One baboon finally said to the other, 'Does this mean that we have to start it all over again?' "

Senator Everett Dirksen of Illinois was an outstanding public speaker, whether he was reading from a text or speaking off the cuff. His voice was so melodious that one could almost visualize syrup oozing as the words rolled out.

I once had a chance meeting with Senator Dirksen on an Armistice Day in the early 1960s. It was a custom in Chicago to have an Armistice Day ceremony at 11 a.m. on November 11 at Madison and State Streets in the heart of the Loop.

I was assigned to cover the ceremony and, arriving a little early, I went into a nearby drugstore for a cup of coffee. I was sitting on a stool at the counter when a man slid onto the stool next to me. It was Dirksen.

To make conversation, I observed it was a rather chilly day but that the senator did not have a hat.

"I have gotten used to not wearing hats," Dirksen said. "I used to always wear a hat, but every time I appeared at a Republican meeting, I found that my hat was missing when I left.

"Later, I learned that my hat had been raffled off to help raise funds for the party. That was certainly a good cause, but I really felt that I was losing too many hats, so I decided to go bare-headed."

Senator Hubert Humphrey of Minnesota was another champion public speaker.

I recall covering Senator Humphrey at a luncheon. Before the luncheon began, several of us took him aside for a short interview. After talking for a few minutes, Humphrey suddenly stopped and said, "I'd like to start this all over again because I don't really know much about what I was saying."

Instead of being irritated by such a false start, all of us appreciated Humphrey's candor. I wonder if a political leader today could get away with such frankness without being slammed by the media.

The hardest speeches to cover usually were those given off the cuff without any prepared text. Such speeches often consisted mostly of fragmentary sentences even though it sounded good to the audiences.

I have never forgotten the trouble I had in writing a story about a speech given by Senator Joseph McCarthy, the controversial Wisconsin senator, who was eventually censored by the Senate for his unbridled anti-Communist attacks on people in the federal government.

McCarthy was speaking to a luncheon meeting of the Chicago Bar Association, and his demagogic speech brought frequent bursts of loud applause. My notes, however, were mostly of fragmentary sentences.

For instance, I recall his saying that "we must give Communist China an ultimatum or else," as he brought his fist down with a bang on the lectern.

There's no way of knowing what McCarthy meant by "or else." Did he mean that we should start a war and drop the bomb on China?

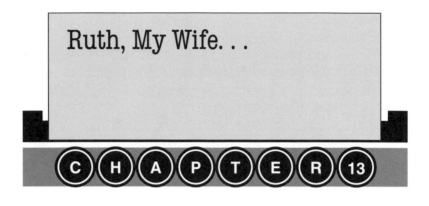

Ruth, My Wife. . .

CHAPTER 13

My wife, Ruth, and I met at the *Tribune,* and I will never forget that first day.

For some time I had seen her at a distance, when she was editor of a very excellent employees' magazine called *The Little Trib.* But it wasn't until she was transferred to the City Desk as a reporter that I had an opportunity to meet her.

That day I was filling in on the City Hall beat for the regular *Tribune* reporter, Ed Schrieber, who was on vacation. I was in the City Hall pressroom on the second floor when Ruth came in, introduced herself and asked if I could help her.

The city editor had the idea that public employees in the County Building and City Hall were brushing off everyone with no courtesy at all, and he wanted a story showing this.

As I was living with an aunt who owned a house on the Northwest Side of Chicago, and to help Ruth, I told her to use my aunt's address in asking questions. She could use the address for checking on taxes, on assessments, on water bills and other similar services.

Besides being very attractive, Ruth had a charming voice with a wonderful touch of southern accent. I thought she would have a hard time finding anyone in the

County Building or City Hall who would be abrupt or rude to her.

Two hours later, Ruth came back to see me in the pressroom, and she seemed very upset.

"What am I going to do?" she asked. "Everyone was so nice and tried to do everything they could to help me. I was supposed to get a story about all the rude people in the County Building and City Hall."

I suggested that she go in and write the story as she had found it, about how nice people were. I'm sure that she was thrilled, as I was, when her story appeared on the front page of the *Tribune.*

Ruth, who as a journalist used her maiden name of Ruth Moss, worked for the *Tribune* for 50 years as a reporter, writer and editor. Before I moved on to other things, my *Tribune* longevity totaled 33 years, and that included almost five years of military service in World War II.

The best assignment a journalist could have probably would be to cover one's own honeymoon on the expense account. That's what happened to Ruth and me, although we had not planned it that way.

Ruth and I had decided to get married in Europe because she and her mother, Mrs. David Walton Moss, of Dyersburg, Tennessee, had already acquired two places on a tour of six weeks that began with the coronation of Queen Elizabeth II in London in June of 1953. Under the plan, Mrs. Moss' sister, Mrs. William Addison Smith, of Leland, Mississippi, would fly over with me the week before the wedding and then take Ruth's place for the last three weeks of the purchased tour.

We were married in Switzerland in two ceremonies: a civil ceremony on June 15 in Küsnacht, a suburb of Zurich, and an "ecclesiastical consecration" (church wedding) on June 16 in Lucerne. The pastor for our church service was the Rev. Dr. Jean-Jacques von Allmen, a noted theologian whose name I found in a Lucerne telephone directory at the Swiss consulate in Chicago.

After a month of corresponding with various places in Europe, I had found Küsnacht, where one could get married without having to announce banns 30 days in advance. (Küsnacht is German that means "night kiss.")

We were both reporters for the *Chicago Tribune*, and early on the day after our wedding, we received a cablegram from our *Tribune* editor, Don Maxwell. The hotel pageboy at the Grand National Hotel in Lucerne apologized for waking us so early, but he said a cablegram had been sent as an urgent message for immediate delivery.

Maxwell offered to extend our vacation by two weeks and to pay our expenses if we would write a series of three weeks of articles about our honeymoon in Europe.

In the next half-hour, we received two telephone calls— one from Arthur Veysey, head of the *Tribune's* London bureau, and the other from Henry Wales, head of the Paris bureau.

We said that we were very grateful to get the assignment and that we would begin writing in several days. An hour later, Veysey called back and said that Maxwell had cabled again, instructing us to "begin writing at once so that the series could be started in Sunday's paper."

The next thing Ruth and I did was to go shopping—to buy a lightweight portable typewriter, a Hermes. (We still use that Hermes, which has been to the repair shop only once in all these years.)

For our "Honeymoon in Europe," we wrote 21 daily articles. In addition to Switzerland, we traveled by bus, train, air and boat in Germany, France and Italy. At 4 o'clock each afternoon, we telephoned the *Tribune* bureau in London to dictate our daily column for transmission by cable to Chicago.

We made no advance arrangements, getting hotel accommodations at the very last minute. (Traveling without any advance reservations became a habit of ours in many later trips to Europe.)

Ruth Moss Buck, who worked 50 years at the Chicago Tribune *as a writer and editor, shown here when she was an education and feature writer for the* Tribune Sunday Magazine.

For our honeymoon, our expense account with the *Tribune* totaled $1,353.77. That total included $859.03 in general expenses for hotels, meals and incidentals, and $494.74 for transportation expenses in Europe and the cost of telephone calls and cablegrams.

After finishing our articles, we still had about a week to visit several cities, including Geneva, Switzerland. The last two days we planned to spend in Paris.

In Geneva, we took a taxicab late in the afternoon to visit the grounds of the League of Nations. One of the attractions was a lily pond with a constellation dedicated to

President Woodrow Wilson for his leadership in the creation of the League of Nations after World War I.

The lily pond had an irregular edging of slick white marble about a foot wide. Ruth had taken off her shoes and was walking on the edging in stocking feet, which I thought was a very risky thing for her to do.

I walked behind her, feeling very secure in my shoes; but all of a sudden, I slipped and fell into the pond. It was about two feet deep, and I almost went all the way under before getting up. Then I fell a second time.

Turning around, Ruth was obviously so amazed at seeing her husband thrashing around in the lily pond that she couldn't help laughing. Whether her laughter added to my pain, I don't know because I was already in great pain. I had sprained or broken my right foot.

It was almost closing time at the League of Nations grounds, but fortunately a man in a small car came by, and we waved him down. He was a Frenchman, who finally understood our problem and did us a great favor of taking us to our hotel.

Ruth performed excellent emergency service. The gray flannel suit I had been wearing was the only one I had, and Ruth was able to talk the proprietor of a nearby cleaning shop to stay open long enough to dry, clean and press my suit. She also obtained a pair of canes for me because I was almost unable to walk.

Before flying the next day to Paris, I went to a doctor's office, where an X-ray showed my foot was sprained but not broken.

From Paris, we flew to New York City and spent the weekend on Long Island with our good friends, Joan and Cy Clark, and their family.

At the airport in New York City on our way back to Chicago, I was approached by an elderly man who, as it turned out, was interested in my pair of canes.

"You're just back from South Africa?" he asked.

After I had said "No," he explained, "I have never seen canes like that since the Boer War."

I have never been as embarrassed as I was that Monday morning when I returned from our honeymoon to the City Room of the *Tribune* limping along with the two canes.

We have always had a dog in our family. For many years we had poodles, miniature poodles. Then we had a wire-haired fox terrier, a type of dog which I had always wanted since childhood. And now we have a border collie which is the sweetest type of dog one could ever imagine.

With our interest in dogs, it is no wonder that we spotted a tiny dog running down the middle dividing line of a busy expressway in Canada when we were returning from a vacation in late August of 1971. The best way to tell the story is to reprint an article I wrote for the *Chicago Tribune*.

The article had this headline: "The Littlest Dog Wags the Biggest Tail."

My story read as follows:

> The Royal Canadian Mounted Police are everything they are said to be. That's what our family discovered on a vacation trip.
>
> Returning from camping on Prince Edward Island, we were traveling a high-speed highway in New Brunswick, bent on getting home before the Labor Day congestion. Driving our station wagon was Mrs. Buck who is Ruth Moss, a feature writer for the *Tribune*.
>
> All of a sudden, we saw a Chihuahua prancing toward us, right down the white center strip of the highway. Other cars at 70 miles an hour were swerving to avoid hitting the tiny brown dog.
>
> "We've got to save that dog!" exclaimed Ruth, as she brought the car to a quick stop on the black-topped shoulder. Out we all jumped, including daughter and son, Mary Moss and Tom, to flag down cars.
>
> Other motorists joined us in pursuit of the Chihuahua. A few minutes later, Ruth caught the dog, being bitten slightly in doing so. But the dog then readily

curled up in her folded arms as we walked to a nearby farmhouse.

"I don't know what to tell you to do," said a young mother at the farmhouse. "It came up to our house without a collar on last night, but I had to let it out this morning after it had snapped at one of the children."

There was nothing to do but to take the dog with us. The dog settled into Ruth's lap and then climbed to her shoulder to lick her face, as she was trying to drive.

Five miles farther along, we spotted a sign and turned off the super highway to a small New Brunswick town, Petitcodiac. There we found a station of the Royal Canadian Mounted Police.

"Most Chihuahuas are owned by ladies who love them very much," Ruth told the desk sergeant, disclosing an insight about which none of the others in our family was aware.

"If you can't find the woman who owns this dog, telephone us collect in Evanston, Illinois, and let us know," Ruth added, "because we would be glad to give it a home."

"Don't worry, madam—we have handled cases like this before," assured the desk sergeant, as he took our telephone number and address. Before we left, the dog was turned over to a squad car officer, who was instructed first to make an inquiry in the area where we had found the dog.

A day or so ago, we received a letter from the "J" Division of the Royal Canadian Mounted Police at Petitcodiac. The letter:

"Dear Sir,

"I felt that you would be interested in the disposition of the dog you found in this area. The owner, Mrs. Rosella Craig of 79 Winter Street, St. John, New Brunswick, had lost the dog in the Sussex area while on a trip, and it had been brought to this area by a second party who, in turn, lost it again.

"Mrs. Craig has since taken possession of the dog. Thanking you for your kindness I am

Yours truly,

G. G. Leahy, CPL. No. 19669
The Petitcodiac"

A telephone call by us to Mrs. Craig in St. John revealed that the Chihuahua, which is named Bimbo, is the only dog she and her husband Frederick, a utility company employee, and their five children had ever owned.

"Bimbo was given to me 11 years ago by my late brother-in-law," said Mrs. Craig. "All of us nearly went crazy when Bimbo disappeared."

The dog was believed to have been picked up by hitch-hikers near the Craig's summer cottage at Sussex, two days before we found it near Petitcodiac, about 25 miles away.

After inquiring at a Royal Canadian Mounted Police station, Mrs. Craig reclaimed Bimbo on Labor Day at an animal hospital near Moncton, where Corporal Leahy had taken it for safekeeping.

Everyone should see Las Vegas at one time or another if nothing more than to satisfy one's curiosity. That's what Ruth and I did after a friend gave us this advice:

"While you're here in Los Angeles, you should drive to Las Vegas to see Sodom and Gomorrah before they fall."

This suggestion was made to Ruth and me by Will Parks, a Tennessean who also was visiting his daughter, Caroline, and her husband, Bruce.

"And you will have no trouble getting a room," said Caroline. "Just telephone Hickman Benson, who is assistant manager of the Stardust Hotel. He's from Dyersburg, and he will be happy to take care of you."

Dyersburg, Tennessee, happens to be Ruth's hometown.

I immediately got Hickman on the phone, and he assured us that he would have a good room for us.

"But we don't want anything fancy. Something like a double bed would do."

Late the next afternoon we waited in a long line at the Stardust to check in. Hickman, as the assistant manager, had taken over helping to register people.

When we finally reached him, he treated us as kissing cousins.

"Besides meeting you, this also is a great day for me because our poodle has just had puppies," he said. "I'm awfully sorry, but you will have to be a little patient about the double bed. It will take us some time to find one, but we will get it."

I tried my best to explain to Hickman that my reference to a double bed was merely a figure of speech to indicate that we didn't want anything too expensive.

An hour later there was a knock on the door of our room. Two men came in and replaced our twin beds with a double bed.

Later that evening we happened to meet his wife, Hallie Benson, who worked in the casino of the Sands Hotel.

"Did Hickman get you the double bed?" she asked. "I was sure he would because we never let anyone from Dyersburg down."

Incidentally, Mr. Will Parks, who was 95 years old at that time, lived as a spry person to three months short of his 105th birthday.

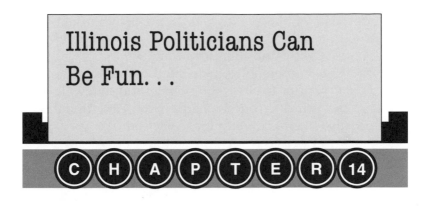

Illinois Politicians Can Be Fun...

CHAPTER 14

As a *Chicago Tribune* reporter for more than 30 years, I became acquainted with many politicians after they had been elected to office—but not before, with one exception. I covered only one political campaign, and that was a campaign I shall never forget.

In the fall of 1954, I was assigned to cover what was called the Republican Campaign Caravan. This involved three nominees: Joseph T. Meek, candidate for United States senator; Vernon L. Nickell, running for reelection as superintendent of public instruction; and Warren Wright, candidate for state treasurer.

Meek was not really a politician, although he was a very outspoken conservative. He had won the nomination in a primary battle with seven other candidates. He was a very sincere person with very straight-laced habits. He neither smoked nor drank, and his only fault seemed to be that he couldn't pass a Dairy Queen without stopping.

Nickell was a veteran in both education and politics. His homely features and height of 6 feet 4 inches caused his friends to think of him as a modern-day Abraham Lincoln.

Wright, by contrast, wore a white hat and spoke in a slightly nasal monotone, so that he was often called a Will Rogers. He was frequently misidentified as his namesake, the late head of the prestigious Kentucky thoroughbred horseracing stable, Calumet Farm. Wright, the politician, never corrected this misidentification.

The *Tribune*, although supporting the Republicans, also assigned a reporter to cover the Democratic statewide candidates, the principal one being Senator Paul Douglas, a very popular liberal running for reelection. We were given equal space in each day's *Tribune*, about one column each, and the real problem was finding something new to write about every day.

Wright had very little to say, but what he said was very effective from his standpoint. One of his stock statements was, "I want to be state treasurer so bad I can taste it. In fact, I just can't wait until I get my hands on all that money."

That comment never failed to produce a wave of chuckles.

Wright's campaign speeches mostly consisted of long jokes and other anecdotes designed to amuse the crowd without burdening anyone with substantive ideas. For example, he would add a closing line such as: "Now when I'm elected state treasurer, I want you all to come to Springfield to see me. I will take you down into the vault and let you hold one million dollars. The only thing is, when you leave, you have to drop the one million dollars."

At each town where there was a bank, however, while Meek and Nickell were speaking to an audience, Wright would go his own way and spend his time visiting the local banker. He would tell the banker that when he became treasurer, he would deposit some of the state funds in that bank.

The Republican Campaign Caravan touched every part of Illinois in the seven weeks before the election on the first Tuesday of November. In September through October 15, the Republicans visited 96 of the state's 102 counties, with crowded days beginning with breakfast meetings and ending late in the evening.

We got home for a break late Saturday and were off again late Sunday afternoon. The last two weeks were spent in Chicago and the six-county metropolitan area.

As the Republican caravan consisting of three station wagons entered a town, the sound truck in the lead would be driven by one of Wright's long-time political friends, Gabby Miller of Springfield. As the caravan moved along, Gabby would be on the loud speaker telling people about the approach of the Republican candidates and inviting everyone to come down to the town square to meet them.

During the campaign the Eisenhower Administration in Washington was keeping an eye on Joe Meek, particularly because there was a need for another good Republican vote in the Senate. In support of the campaign, several representatives of the administration came to Illinois to help Meek.

One night in Mattoon, the secretary of agriculture, Ezra Benson, showed up unexpectedly to address a crowd of farmers. On two other occasions, Richard Nixon, who was vice president, came to Illinois to speak on behalf of Joe Meek. The first time, Nixon spoke on a warm, sunny day on the campus of the University of Illinois in Urbana. He was a very effective speaker, as I recall, and students crowded around him, while some were hanging out of windows to listen.

Because of the administration's interest in Joe Meek, the campaign in Illinois also attracted the attention of columnists and newspaper correspondents from Washington. A nationally known columnist, Joseph Alsop, joined us late one evening in Southern Illinois.

The next morning began with a breakfast meeting in the courthouse, but after only five minutes or so, Alsop told me that he was getting bored, and he suggested we go out and learn what the people thought.

I went with Alsop as he entered a tavern just off the town square. At the bar there were several farmers on stools who were chasing early morning shots of whiskey with beer and picking their teeth with straw. Alsop was a somewhat effeminate-looking person who was dressed in a Brooks Brothers suit and spoke with a very clipped English accent.

As Alsop approached the farmers and started asking questions, they seemed to be completely mystified as to what kind of a person he was. I thought he might be in a little danger of insulting these people, but instead, after a few minutes of his persistence in asking questions, the farmers began talking with him.

The next week, Alsop wrote a devastating national column about Joe Meek, comparing him to Willy Loman in the play, "Death of a Salesman." Meek was far better than a Willy Loman and, in fact, was really almost too honest and forthright to be a successful politician.

The Eisenhower Administration undoubtedly was disappointed in the outcome. Senator Paul Douglas was very popular at that time, and Meek had no chance at all of beating him. He lost by a wide margin.

The other two Republicans did very well. Vernon Nickell won re-election as superintendent of public instruction without difficulty, and Warren Wright won election as state treasurer by a big margin.

As state treasurer, Wright was to play an important role in the investigation of Orville Hodge, the state auditor who was later convicted of misappropriating more than a million dollars of state funds. Hodge diverted state money to his own personal use by submitting phony vouchers for which the treasurer's office issued checks.

Under the normal procedure, the vouchers and returned checks would go back to Hodge's auditor office as the only record for safekeeping. However, perhaps driven by political jealousy and ambition, Wright kept an extra, secret record of the vouchers by having them microfilmed before they were returned to Hodge's office. Wright's microfilm of Hodge's phony vouchers turned out to be critical evidence in the investigation.

The sheriff of Cook County once was considered a dead-end political office.

If the sheriff weren't dishonest, the public seemed to think he was. The County Jail, of which he was the administrator, was often the target of criticism. The sheriff's police force for unincorporated areas was criticized from time to time as being dishonest or plainly inefficient. To the public, the sheriff usually stood out as a distinctive personality.

During World War II, there was so much gambling in the unincorporated area that the sheriff, Thomas O'Brien, was known as "Blind Tom."

Richard J. Daley, who later was to become Chicago's mayor, ran for sheriff as the Democratic candidate in 1946, but was soundly defeated. It probably was one of the best things that ever happened to him. There was no question about Daley's personal honesty, but the taint of the sheriff's office could well have ruined his political career.

The Republican who defeated Daley was Elmer Michael Walsh, under whom, in the early part of World War II, I had served as an investigator in the Provost Marshal's Office in Chicago. As an Army captain, Walsh had been the head of the investigative staff.

Shortly after taking office as sheriff, Walsh became engaged in a fight with a hard-hitting veteran *Tribune* reporter, James Doherty, who had a reputation for being somewhat overbearing.

The fight began after Walsh appointed and then fired his sheriff's police chief, who happened to be one of Doherty's closest friends.

The fight became so bitter that Walsh let it be known that he trusted only two *Tribune* reporters and that they were the only ones he would talk with. One of the reporters was Ed Kennedy, whom he had known since grade school. I was the other one because of my service with him in the Army.

When Walsh became sheriff, I was in the Financial News Department of the *Tribune*, and when the city editor wanted to ask Walsh something, I often was assigned to making the trip to the County Building to interview him.

Among the sheriffs I covered, John Babb, a lawyer, was the most flamboyant. He took on a cowboy style of behavior by wearing a pearl-handled revolver in a holster on his hip.

Frank Sain moved up from warden of the County Jail to become the sheriff and he couldn't resist bringing a memento with him. As a special attraction, Sain displayed a replica of an electric chair in his sheriff's office. Capital punishment was imposed at some frequency then, and the executions were carried out in a theater-type room in the basement of the jail with the warden in charge.

An especially serious approach was brought to the sheriff's office with the election in 1954 of a scholar, Joseph Lohman, who had been a professor of sociology and criminal justice at the University of Chicago.

In an apparent attempt to help rehabilitate the inmates, Sheriff Lohman encouraged everyone in the jail to devote any free moments to reading. For one thing, Lohman eliminated a long-standing practice of censoring the daily newspapers delivered to the jail.

"The prisoners used to get newspapers that were full of holes," he explained. "The model prisoners, who were known as 'trustees,' were given the job of clipping out articles considered unfit for prisoners to read. We learned, however, that the 'trustees' often sold the censored clippings to the prisoners on the side.

"The news about the jail may not be too good at times, but we are making the papers available without censorship just the same," Lohman said in announcing his reading program.

As another important feature of the reading program, Lohman created a circulating library at the jail and asked for contributions of books by the public.

Much as he disliked censorship, Sheriff Lohman admitted that he had to step in to disqualify one of the first books contributed for the new library. The book, from an anonymous donor, was entitled *You Can Escape*.

In the mid-1960s, Richard B. Ogilvie became one of a few sheriffs to go on to higher political positions. After serving as sheriff, Ogilvie was first elected president of the Cook County Board and then governor of Illinois.

Also moving up after serving as sheriff following Ogilvie was Joseph Woods, who became a member of the Cook County Board. Woods, a former chief investigator for the Better Government Association, was a brother of Rosemary Woods, the personal secretary to President Richard Nixon. Since they were the same size, Woods took great pride in being the recipient of Nixon's hand-me-down blue serge suits.

Mayor Daley—Richard J., frequently referred to as "the original Mayor Daley"—was not the typical politician of his day.

At that time politics in Chicago was a freewheeling game. Many politicians went out of their way to court newspaper people as friends, expecting favorable coverage as a result. In political circles Christmastime was a big season for remembering friends with all sorts of gifts, such as whiskey, wine and gift certificates. Daley, however, was known to send only Christmas cards.

Unlike many of his companions in the Democratic Party, Richard J. Daley was not exactly an outgoing person. He was friendly, but not too friendly.

He was very neat and was always dressed in a well-pressed blue suit with white shirt and tie. He was extremely proper, never smoked and was never known to drink in public.

Daley was known to be a deeply religious man, starting every day by attending Mass at his parish church, partly (it was said) in memory of his parents.

Earl Bush, his press secretary and a Jew, recalls that Daley was also highly respectful of other people's religion.

"I can never forget the time I was in his office on Yom Kippur," recalls Bush. "The mayor told me I should leave his office and get to the synagogue."

As a Tribune *reporter, Tom Buck (right) began covering former Mayor Richard J. Daley from the time Daley became Cook County clerk.*

Daley was always very polite, but he seemed to keep a distance, especially from reporters. It seemed that he never really trusted the news media. A newly elected Democratic official once told me about getting advice from Daley on how to conduct himself. Among other things, he said Daley told him that he knew of only two or three reporters who could be trusted.

At press conferences Daley was usually very forthright, although reporters used tape recorders and afterwards listened to the tapes very closely to make sure they understood what he had said.

If he wanted to avoid an answer, he had a very disarming way of doing so. This was particularly true if the reporter asking the question was knowledgeable about the subject and seemed to be probing a little bit too deeply. In such instances Daley would say, "You know more about that than I do," and move to the next subject.

As a *Tribune* reporter covering the County Building, I got to know Richard J. Daley when he was Cook County clerk, which was several years before he became mayor. The clerk's office produced very little news since it was involved primarily with administrative functions, such as conducting suburban elections and issuing marriage licenses.

One day the secretary to a top executive at the *Tribune* called me in the County Building pressroom and asked if I could help the executive's daughter and her fiancé get a marriage license. I said that the couple should see me in the County Building pressroom, and I would help them get their license without any delay.

I called Daley just to ask how we could avoid a long waiting line, and he said, "Bring them in to see me." I said I didn't want to bother him, but he insisted that I bring the couple to his office.

He greeted them very warmly and called in an employee who was known for his expert penmanship. He then had the marriage license written by hand, after which he gave the couple a little talk on how wonderful it was to be married and to have children.

He told them how much Mrs. Daley and he enjoyed their seven children. On a table behind his desk was a large framed montage of photographs of the Daley family. Daley obviously enjoyed issuing marriage licenses, and I later brought in several other couples for their licenses.

In June of 1953, Ruth (who was also a *Tribune* reporter) and I were married in Switzerland. The first day I was back on the job in the County Building, I received a call from Daley.

"What's wrong with my marriage licenses?" asked Daley. "You didn't have to go all the way to Switzerland to get a license."

I think he was kidding, but I really wasn't quite sure.

In the early 1960s, Earl Bush, the mayor's press secretary, decided to get Daley acquainted with the intellectual community. He scheduled him to speak at several university functions, the foremost of which was the Law School Forum at Harvard University in Cambridge, Massachusetts.

The forum was scheduled for a Friday evening, and I drew the assignment to cover Daley's appearance there. Ruth went along with me, and we checked into the Copley Plaza Hotel, where Daley and his party also were staying. Among those with him was his son, Richard M. Daley, now the Chicago mayor, who had come from Providence, Rhode Island, where he was attending college, to hear his father speak at the Harvard Law School Forum.

More than 500 people were on hand for the forum, which was held in a large auditorium near the Harvard campus. The subject was urban problems, and appearing with Daley were two Harvard professors.

Each speaker gave a 10-minute opening statement. Like many politicians, Daley couldn't read a written speech very well, and his opening remarks made a very poor impression. In fact, some people in the audience were heard to murmur such things as, "I told you so; he's just a politician."

It was an entirely different story when the questioning from the audience began. Daley was very good at fielding questions, and he was in rare form that evening. There were nothing but hardball questions, and Daley was so good in his answers that the two Harvard professors just sat back and listened. I had a feeling that Daley was like a good baseball shortstop, catching hard-hit grounders with perfect ease.

After more than a half hour of such questioning, Daley had so successfully enlightened the audience about urban problems that everyone jumped up and gave him a big burst of applause. He could have been elected the mayor of Boston the next day.

Later, at the hotel, Daley told me that he and his party were going to be given a tour of the Harvard campus the next day, and he invited me to come along. In the morning I was at the Copley Plaza front desk waiting with Mayor Daley for others to come down when he asked me, "Why aren't you taking that job at the Chicago Transit Authority?"

I was dumbfounded. I had been contacted by the CTA board about taking a public relations job, but it was supposed to be a secret.

"I didn't know that you knew anything about that," I replied.

"Oh, I know about it," said Daley. "Why aren't you taking it?"

I felt that Daley might have been a little bit upset about my hesitancy, and I thought for a moment how I could make an explanation without hurting his feelings.

I said that I very much liked being a newspaperman, and I felt that, if possible, one should like his job and that the worst thing in the world would be to have to work at something one didn't like. I said further that I thought I would like the public relations work at the Chicago Transit Authority, but I wasn't sure.

Daley responded, "I think it's very important to like what you're doing. I told my boys that it was up to them to decide what to do, but that I wanted them to be sure their work was honorable and that they liked what they were doing. Also, I told them that whatever they do they should do the best, and if they wanted to run a filling station in Chicago, that's fine. Except it would have to be the best filling station in Chicago."

Not long after that I had another personal experience with Mayor Daley. My wife, Ruth, and I had a fine pediatrician, Dr. John J. Reichert, for our two children, Mary and Tom. One Saturday when we took the children to see Dr. Reichert, he asked me if I knew Mayor Daley. I explained that I saw him once in a while on assignments and asked him why he had asked the question.

Dr. Reichert, who was very active with the Chicago Medical Society, said that his organization, at the mayor's request, had submitted his (Dr. Reichert's) name as a nominee for appointment to the Chicago Board of Education. Dr. Reichert explained that he could not take such a job because of his age and his desire to retire.

Dr. Reichert explained further that his name had been submitted solely as a stop-gap step so that the medical society would be sure to have a representative on the school board. He said that the medical society planned to submit the name of the intended appointee in a few days.

Dr. Reichert asked if it would be possible for me to tell Mayor Daley about the medical society's plan to submit another nominee. I said that I could not promise anything, but if I saw the mayor, I would pass along his message.

On Wednesday of the next week, I just happened to be on the fifth floor near the mayor's office when Mayor Daley was going to lunch. The mayor had a practice of slipping out a side door and then darting to a waiting elevator to get out of the building before anyone could see or talk with him.

He practically ran into me on his way to the elevator, and I said, "Mayor Daley, could I have a word with you?"

"What's up?" asked the mayor.

I said I wanted to talk to him just a few minutes about Dr. John Reichert.

"What's wrong with him?" asked the mayor.

I replied, "Nothing. He's a great doctor."

"Fine," said the mayor. "I'll appoint him."

And before I had a chance to say anything further, the mayor was in the elevator and on his way out to lunch.

Later that afternoon, Mayor Daley announced the appointment of Dr. John Reichert to the Chicago School Board. When I heard about it, I immediately called Dr. Reichert to apologize and to explain how I had failed. Dr. Reichert accepted the appointment and served on the board for several years before retiring.

When the present mayor, Richard M. Daley, was first elected to the mayor's office in 1989, I wrote an article about how his election had given Chicago the unique historical distinction of having had two sets of father-son mayors. Mayor Richard M. Daley is the eldest son of the late Mayor Richard J. Daley, whose service of more than 21 years was terminated by a fatal heart attack on December 20, 1976.

In 1879, the first of two Carter Henry Harrisons began a father-son dynasty in City Hall when the elder Carter H. Harrison was elected to the first of five terms as mayor. The mayoral term then was only for two years, and the first Mayor Harrison served four consecutive terms. After a lapse, he came back for a fifth term in time to be the city's official host for the World's Columbian Exposition of 1893.

He was destined, however, to serve only about seven months of that final term. He was shot to death by a deranged office-seeker on October 28, 1893, a few days before the Exposition closed.

The son, Carter H. Harrison, Jr., was first elected mayor in April of 1897. He served four two-year terms and one four-year term for a total of 12 years.

Accounts of the political and public service activities of the Harrisons and the Daleys are similar in a number of ways, the foremost being their pronounced love for Chicago.

The day after his election in 1989, Mayor Richard M. Daley appeared on a national television morning show. A New York-based announcer asked him if he was going to be like his father.

"My father loved Chicago and worked very hard, and I will do the same," replied Mayor Richard M. Daley.

Upon his first election, Carter H. Harrison I said, "Chicago is my bride. I love it as a young man loves his chosen one!"

In his autobiography, *Stormy Years*, Carter Harrison, Jr. wrote that "always deep in my inner consciousness" was the ambition to follow in his father's footsteps.

Both Harrisons and both Daleys were graduated from law schools and admitted to the bar. For the most part, however, politics and public service rather than law practice represented their main professional pursuits.

It has been said that no one can beat City Hall because of the insurmountable obstacle of politics combined with bureaucracy.

I had a friend, however, who did beat City Hall; but I could not write a story about it.

If he had to make a choice, Bob Cossum would have chosen boating over eating.

Bob and his wife, Margaret, lived on the shore of Lake Michigan near the landmark Evanston Lighthouse. They had their own pier, which extended about 80 feet into the lake. A sailing boat was Bob's pride and joy, but he also had an old boat with an outboard motor.

In the summer when the lake was calm, Bob used the motor boat for commuting to downtown Chicago. It was the time when the Chicago city government was building the big water filtration plant on landfill just to the north of Navy Pier.

Bob was an executive with a textbook company which had offices in Streeterville, near Navy Pier. It was a 15-mile trip from Bob's pier in Evanston to the Navy Pier area where he tied up his boat in a slip between the pier and the filtration plant construction site.

He had no trouble leaving the boat there all day long— that is, until he bought a brand new boat.

As he was about to tie up the new boat in the slip next to the filtration plant, an official-looking man came rushing over and shouted, "You can't park that boat here. You better get out of here right away and stay out!"

Apparently, the filtration plant boss believed the old boat belonged to one of the workers and that the new boat was owned by an outsider who didn't belong there.

For the next week, Margaret told me, Bob was "completely down in the dumps" because he had to drive instead of taking the boat to work.

"Then, on Saturday morning, he seemed to have had a bright idea," she recalled. "He spent the whole day with a tarpaulin, some stencils, and a can of white paint."

With utmost confidence, Bob set out early Monday morning in his new motor boat headed for Chicago. As he was tying up in the slip, the construction boss saw him and came running over and was about to say something when Bob pulled the tarpaulin over the boat.

"Don't worry, we'll keep an eye on the boat for you," said the construction boss as he saw what was on the tarpaulin.

The lettering, in large white letters on the gray tarpaulin, read: CLEAN WATER FOR CHICAGO — MAYOR RICHARD J. DALEY.

There was no doubt Bob had beaten City Hall, but I couldn't write a story, much as I wanted to. It would have given him away.

In the "Front Page" days of the 1920s, newspapers developed a habit of playing hardball with county and city officials. Under this get-tough policy, the papers sometimes insisted on having direct telephone lines into the offices of the public officials, thereby avoiding any delays caused by having to go through switchboards and secretaries.

When I covered the County Building in the 1950s, there were still instances in which newspapers had such direct lines. John Boyle, a Democrat from Oak Park, who was Cook County state's attorney, was one such official to whom the *Tribune* had a direct line.

Colonel Robert R. McCormick, the editor and publisher of the *Tribune*, was in the hospital for a routine physical checkup when he called his secretary and told her to ask Doyle, one of the *Tribune's* barbers, to come to the hospital to give him a shave and a haircut.

The Colonel's secretary called the *Tribune* operators to relay the message to the barber shop, but the *Tribune* operator handling the call apparently was fairly new on the job. Instead of plugging in to the barber, Doyle, she put the call through to Boyle, the state's attorney.

State's Attorney Boyle, who was known to have a quick temper, was in the midst of a serious conference; but when the *Tribune* direct line rang, he picked up the phone.

Over the direct wire came the *Tribune* operator's voice:

"Mr. Boyle, please go over to Passavant Hospital right away, and give Colonel McCormick a shave and a haircut."

"What in the hell are you talking about?" sputtered Boyle.

I heard about the incident through the County Building grapevine, but I wondered if there was any truth to it. When I next saw Boyle, that was the first thing I asked.

Boyle said, "That's exactly what happened. I was so damn mad I almost pulled the phone out of the wall."

It didn't help any that the *Tribune* at that time was criticizing Boyle very severely about the way his office had handled a controversial case.

With Dan Ryan as president and John Duffy as chairman of its finance committee, the Cook County Board in the 1950s was pretty well controlled by the Irish. But that didn't keep other ethnic board members from trying to get their piece of the action.

On March 9, 1955, a resolution was introduced at a County Board meeting making March 17th a holiday for any employee wishing to pay homage to St. Patrick.

The resolution was introduced not by an Irishman but by Commissioner Edward "Michael" Sneed, the only African-American member of the board.

Sneed's resolution had become a tradition. It was the 15th year that he had introduced the St. Patrick's resolution. As in the past, most of the county's 9,500 employees would become Irish and take the day off, Commissioner Sneed predicted.

On this occasion, though, Commissioner Sneed's resolution was not the only action concerning holidays. Sponsored by Commissioner Arthur X. Elrod, a second resolution set aside April 7 and 8 as days off for Jewish employees to observe the Passover.

Until then, other board members had held their tongues about holidays. But they could keep still no longer.

"What about the Swedes, Danes, Norwegians, and everyone else?" they shouted.

Commissioner William N. Erickson announced that in June he would sponsor a resolution giving employees of Swedish descent a day off for the observance of Swedish Pioneer Day.

Commissioner Chris A. Jensen said he had plans for a resolution for Danish Independence Day, also in June.

As an observer, Andy Petersen, assistant purchasing agent, said he would like the board to consider a resolution early in October for the observance of Leif Erickson Day.

The discussion about holidays came to an end when Commissioner Charles F. Chaplin, a new member of the board and a life member of the St. Andrew's Society of Illinois, announced that in November he would sponsor a resolution for St. Andrew's Day. Chaplin then startled everyone by adding:

"And in keeping with the high principles of the patron saint of Scotland, that will be a day of work."

My story carried the headline: " 'Holiday Spirit' Swamps Board—County Commissioners Start with St. Pat."

It may have sounded corny, but it was a pleasant interlude to an otherwise dull County Board meeting.

From President Truman to Vice President Nixon. . .

C H A P T E R 15

The *Chicago Tribune* became famous in November of 1948 for printing its early home edition with the headline, "Dewey Defeats Truman," even though there were no election returns to justify that statement. The editors had gambled on the polls which predicted that Truman didn't have a chance.

They lost that gamble, and the photograph of Truman holding up the *Tribune* front page with the erroneous headline became the lasting image of that presidential election.

The *Tribune* was not the only publication to get it wrong. Almost a week later, *Life* magazine carried a billboard on its cover featuring a portrait of Dewey with the headline, "Our Next President." Magazine production lead times were longer then, and *Life,* too, had gambled with a preprinted edition.

Truman's success may have been based in part on his genuine understanding of people and his distaste for spoilsport rules, as the following story illustrates.

Shortly after the 1948 Presidential election, I heard a story second- or third-hand that happened in Logansport, Indiana, near my hometown of Star City. I wasn't sure if the story was true because it sounded like something that someone could have made up. Years later, quite by accident, I found out that it really was true.

First, the story.

Logansport, which is about 130 miles south and east of Chicago, is an historic location where the Eel River joins the Wabash River. There was a large railroad passenger station in the downtown area. Next to the railway tracks was a long strip of old Victorian houses and beyond that was the river.

The strip of old homes was notorious as a red-light district.

A large crowd had spilled over the railway tracks to hear Truman, who was campaigning from the rear of his whistle-stop train. As he was speaking, he seemed to be looking straight into one of the large Victorian houses.

When he finished his speech, he had one final comment.

"My good friends of Logansport and Indiana, I'm sorry to have to leave," he said, "because from what I can see here, I certainly would like to stay around a while."

That brought a roar of laughter from the audience, and Truman looked rather perplexed, not knowing why he had gotten such a response to his standard "departure" line.

He had, of course, unknowingly been looking straight at the front door of one of the biggest houses in the red-light district.

Verification of this story came this way.

I am a member of a great old Chicago club, the Cliff Dwellers, which is a luncheon and dinner club with a membership of men and women who are mostly engaged or interested in the visual arts, architecture, literature and music. Many of the waiters have been former employees of the Pullman Railway dining cars.

One of the features of the Cliff Dwellers is a members' table where one may join other members for luncheon and for a good session of storytelling. One day I told the story I had heard about Truman's Logansport whistle stop.

I didn't realize it, but one of our waiters, known as Traveler, was listening in. As I finished the story, Traveler spoke up.

"That's right, Mr. Buck. That's right. I know it happened because I was there and heard it."

Traveler then explained that he had worked on the whistle-stop train which was provided by the Baltimore and Ohio Railroad.

"That was one of the best times I ever had with the Pullman Company," he said. "It was great working on the Truman train because it was a lot of fun."

He went on to say that he and other members of the crew often rolled dice or shot craps behind the train while Truman was giving his speeches.

"We got away with this for a long while," said Traveler. "But one day, one of the Secret Service men, who was something of a jerk in our opinion, caught us and told us that the next time we rolled dice or shot craps he would have us arrested by the local sheriff."

For the next several days it was pretty gloomy on the train—so much so that President Truman finally asked what was wrong.

"One of us got up enough nerve to tell him what had happened. The next day the Secret Service man who had threatened us disappeared, and we learned that he had been sent out to Arizona. We got the message okay, and from then on, we shot craps every time a stop was made."

I had yet another encounter with the Truman legacy.

Early in October of 1957, I had an interesting assignment that took me to Kansas City, Missouri. I was to cover a Monday civic luncheon meeting celebrating a large urban renewal program for the city.

It was a time when many people were still traveling by rail, and I had a very comfortable overnight trip, arriving in Kansas City early on Sunday afternoon.

I had reserved a room at the Muehlebach Hotel in downtown Kansas City. The Muehlebach was an old hotel that had been enlarged by a modern addition built during the administration of President Truman. The larger hotel was needed to house the traveling press corps and others going to Kansas City when Truman went home to the suburb of Independence.

The first thing I noticed in my hotel room was a very large bowl of fruit on the coffee table. There were apples, oranges, peaches, bananas and grapes. As I was picking up a bunch of grapes, I noticed a small bottle in the bowl. Then I saw a second bottle.

One bottle was a half-pint of good Scotch, and the other was a half-pint of bourbon.

I called the desk clerk and said, "You must have made a mistake. I didn't order any Scotch or bourbon."

"That's for you, compliments of the Muehlebach," said the clerk. "You see, Kansas City is dry on Sundays, and when we know the person arriving is a newspaperman, we always put the bowl of fruit with the Scotch and bourbon in the room. We started that policy when Truman was President and we had many from the press here, often arriving on Sunday."

One of the things I learned in my years of covering politicians is that despite how honest and well-intentioned a public official may be, he or she can be tarred by scandal over which they had no control or knowledge.

Such was the case of Adlai E. Stevenson who served one term as governor of Illinois and later ran twice unsuccessfully as the Democratic candidate for President against Dwight Eisenhower.

There was no more honest man than Stevenson, but during his four years as governor, he was twice embarrassed by scandal.

First, his campaign manager and executive secretary, James W. Mulroy, resigned at Stevenson's request when it was discovered that as an insider Mulroy had bought stock in a racing track at 5 cents a share.

However, the scandal that hurt Stevenson the most—while benefiting me— involved the sale of horsemeat as hamburger in the Chicago area. The sale of horsemeat had been allowed by Charles W. Wray, the state superintendent of food and dairies. He was fined for taking a $3,500 bribe which allowed the horsemeat sale.

Federal price controls were still in effect, and I received a tip on the horsemeat scandal from Michael J. Howlett, a prominent upcoming Democrat who was regional director of price control for the federal government.

As a result, I got the first exclusive story on the horsemeat scandal for the *Tribune* and won a $100 bonus.

The scandal had a wide impact in the Chicago area. People thought a second time before ordering hamburger meat, and there was a noticeable decline in the demand for hamburgers at restaurants.

Horsemeat was used in the manufacture of some dog food, and one manufacturer became so concerned about the negative effect of the horsemeat scandal that a press conference was called in Chicago.

It was organized by Frank Wharton, vice president of the Ken-L Products Division of the Quaker Oats Company. His objective was to clear the name of horsemeat as animal food.

I wrote the *Tribune's* story on the press conference, beginning with these two paragraphs:

"The Chicago Athletic Association, 12 S. Michigan Ave., yesterday barred 8 pounds of horsemeat and four newspaper photographers from a press conference called to explain the use of horsemeat in the dog food industry.

"Photographers were kept out by a club rule of long standing: They're just not welcome. The rule against anyone bringing in horsemeat stemmed from an emergency."

One of Wharton's colleagues, John Christiansen, superintendent of the Ken-L dog food plant in Rockford, had been stopped at the door and asked about a large package he was carrying.

Informed that the package contained horsemeat, the doorman summoned the manager of the CAA, George Slossos, who took a firm stand.

"I don't think this is an appropriate time for anyone to bring horsemeat in here, what with the horsemeat scandal making the headlines," said Slossos.

Wharton apologized to us reporters and explained that he had planned to offer us either horsemeat steaks or beef steaks at a luncheon.

Apparently, unbeknown to the CAA management, Wharton—a member of the Association for many years— had often entertained a dozen special friends with good government-inspected horsemeat steaks in room 1201, which he described as "a little club within a club."

Instead of having a choice that day, we reporters were treated to beef steaks at the press luncheon.

During my years covering government in Chicago, there usually was a major controversy or scandal taking place in the Cook County Building or City Hall.

For everyday routine stories, all of us in the pressroom worked together and filled in for others when they couldn't cover a story. It was different, though, when it came to controversies and scandals. In those cases, everyone was on his or her own, often trying to get scoops or exclusives.

Early in 1952, there was a scandal in the Cook County government that became an influential factor in the election of an Illinois governor.

A prominent Evanston Republican, William N. Erickson, who was president of the Cook County Board, was considered to be the leading Republican candidate for governor. In Cook County he was supported by all the Republican committeemen with one exception. The exception was a Chicago Republican ward committeeman, Charles Fleck, who supported an up-and-coming young Republican, William G. Stratton.

Stratton, who was state treasurer, was considered a long shot. In addition to Erickson as the favorite, there were three other older Republicans who had announced their intentions of running in the gubernatorial primary.

However, it took only one telephone call, reportedly from the office of Charles Fleck, to knock Erickson out of the race.

That telephone call, which was made to the City Desk of the *Chicago Daily News*, the major afternoon newspaper, brought to light a ghost payroller on the administrative staff of the County Board president, Erickson.

The payroller, as explained in the exclusive *Daily News* story, was a state representative, James Adduci, representing Chicago's West Side. Adduci was listed on Erickson's staff payroll as James Addison.

No one on Erickson's staff had ever seen him.

Erickson contended that he knew nothing about it. His denial, however, had little or no effect in combating the bad publicity he was getting.

What made matters worse was the fact that, as a state representative, James Adduci was one of a group of West Side legislators known as the "West Side Bloc," which was said to be under the direct influence of the crime syndicate.

After the *Daily News* published the first story, we in the County Building pressroom began figuring out how we could get exclusive stories as a follow-up to the original account.

It occurred to me that a good story might come from an examination of the checks that Adduci had received from the county under the false name of Addison. I asked the county comptroller, Alvin Weber, if he could pull some of the old Adduci or Addison checks from the file.

It was about 10:30 o'clock in the morning when Weber called and said he had found the checks. There were 10 of them, all of them endorsed first by James Addison and then counter-endorsed by James Adduci.

I didn't want the afternoon newspapers to get the story about the checks, so I asked Weber if he would wait until about 4 P.M. to call a press conference to show what he had found. That would keep the afternoon papers from getting too upset with Weber and still give the morning *Tribune,* as well as the morning *Sun-Times,* the exclusive story.

Meanwhile, I had a *Tribune* photographer photograph the checks so we could display them when our first edition came out early in the evening.

Because of the bad publicity, Erickson announced that he no longer had any intention of running for governor. With Committeeman Charles Fleck as his main supporter in Chicago, Stratton won the Republican primary for governor by getting 57 percent of the vote, defeating three other candidates.

That fall Stratton carried 92 counties to win the governorship. He served two terms. A ghost payroll scandal paved the way for him.

Driving in our new Volkswagen Bug, my wife, Ruth, and I accidentally became part of a motorcade for Richard M. Nixon when he was the Republican nominee for President in 1960.

In crashing the motorcade, we had full police protection—to the extent that two policemen watched over our Volkswagen, parked at a fireplug in front of the Drake Hotel on Chicago's Near North Side.

No one ever asked us who we were or what we were doing there, even when we appeared on a stage with Nixon and his wife, Pat, at a reception in the hotel.

With us were three friends—Mr. and Mrs. George A. Seaverns, Jr. and their daughter, Mrs. Clair McNair.

It probably couldn't happen now, particularly with the close Secret Service protection given presidential candidates.

But it did then—on that summer night after the last session of the Republican National Convention was held in the International Amphitheatre at the Union Stock Yards on Chicago's South Side.

We were entertaining the Seaverns and their daughter at the Chicago Press Club, which was then on the top floor of the St. Clair Hotel on Ohio Street one block east of Michigan Avenue.

That night the Press Club was an exciting place, with the presence of many nationally known journalists who had covered the convention.

The acceptance speech by Nixon, who could be seen on television screens in the club, was anticlimactic since everyone had received advanced copies.

When we left the Press Club with the intention of driving our friends to the Chicago & North Western Railroad station so they could catch a train to Lake Forest, Nixon had finished his speech.

It was a tight fit as we all got into the Volkswagen, with Ruth driving. Ohio Street was eastbound, so she had to drive one block north and turn west in Ontario Street.

We had the green light for crossing Michigan Avenue, but Ruth suddenly realized that she had to turn north because Ontario on the west side of Michigan was blocked off.

Moving north on Michigan, we realized that we were in a motorcade behind the last of three limousines. Behind us was the rear guard of the motorcade, consisting of six policemen on motorcycles. Then, realizing the unusual position we were in, Ruth and I told our guests that we should pretend we were part of the Nixon party by saying nothing and acting as if we belonged.

At Walton Place, the motorcade turned east and came to a halt in front of the Drake. As we got out of our Volkswagen at a fireplug, a policeman came running up and said, "Folks, don't worry about your car. We'll be here to watch it."

Ruth and I told our guests to continue acting as if we were part of the Nixon party and to follow us. We fell in directly behind the Nixons as they entered the Drake.

Inside, with the Nixons still immediately in front of us, we did exactly as they did: All of us shook hands with the people who had made a reception aisle towards the stairway. I distinctly remember shaking hands with Nelson Rockefeller and Mrs. Rockefeller, and other leading Republicans. We followed the Nixons up a stairway and then onto a stage in a reception room. Standing directly behind Mr. and Mrs. Nixon, we waved our hands as the audience cheered.

Still, no one thought to ask us who we were. I saw several of our Chicago newspaper friends in the audience, and they looked with amazement, wondering how Ruth and I had gotten there.

For the next half hour, Ruth and our guests enjoyed the reception, partaking of the hors d'oeuvres and refreshing California orange juice. Others were enjoying harder drinks.

When we finally decided to leave, the Seaverns and their daughter, Clair, were shaking their heads with disbelief. How in the world could five complete outsiders suddenly join a presidential candidate and his wife and help them celebrate one of the brightest times of their lives?

Outside the Drake we found the policeman still guarding our Volkswagen at the fireplug. He graciously helped us into the car and wished us a "pleasant good night."

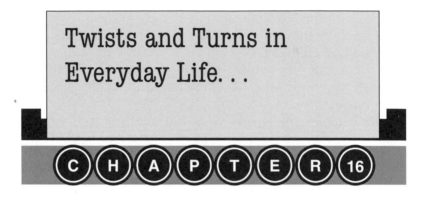

Twists and Turns in Everyday Life...

CHAPTER 16

One of the biggest events in Chicago for many years was the annual International Livestock Exposition held at the International Amphitheatre at the entrance to the Union Stock Yards at 42nd and Halsted streets.

On the Friday after Thanksgiving, the Exposition opened for eight days and nine evenings, attracting more than 400,000 people, of whom more than 50 percent were from Chicago and the suburbs.

The attendance by people from the city and the suburbs was considered to be especially significant because of a need among urban dwellers for greater knowledge of where and how their beefsteaks, pork chops and legs of lamb were produced.

Because of his interest in agriculture, Colonel McCormick asked that a lot of news coverage be given to the International Livestock Exposition.

The farm editor, Dick Orr, was assigned a reporter to help him with the coverage, which amounted to as many as six major stories a day.

In a competition for more than $100,000 in prizes and blue ribbons, which amounted to a lot of money in those days, more than 300 farmers and livestock producers from the United States and Canada brought in exhibits of approximately 5,800 head of cattle, known as "steers," more than 1,500 head of hogs, known as "barrows," and nearly 3,000 head of sheep, known as "wethers." Apart from the regular horse show, there were more than 1,000 horses as livestock competitors.

As a separate attraction, there were horse shows each evening and for five afternoons, featuring competition among 900 harness and saddle horses, hunters, and jumpers and ponies from top stables of the country.

Besides the more than 300 adult farmers competing in the livestock competition, there were also many teenagers from farms, primarily representing 4-H clubs throughout the country. The 4-H club members were interested largely in the junior competition for the steers championship.

In addition to the livestock contests, there also were exhibits and competitions in grain, egg and grain seed.

Many of the 300 exhibitors had been exhibiting at the Exposition for a number of years. One such exhibitor was from Iowa—George Hoffman of Ida Grove. He always brought a carload lot of 25 hogs, and, in addition, generally brought an extra hog to contribute to the USO Club of Chicago. By auctioning the hog, the USO could obtain funds for its work helping military men and women coming through Chicago. Hoffman said he didn't want to have any public credit for making this contribution each year.

In 1952 I had the pleasure of getting the assignment to help Dick Orr at the Livestock Exposition. To me, it was like covering a state fair, which I had once done as a student at Indiana University.

On the first day of the Exposition that year, Dick Orr learned that Hoffman was back with his annual pig for the USO, but that there was something special about it this time. It wasn't just an ordinary pig, but an educated pig that could answer to its name. It had been named Eddie after Hoffman's father.

Eddie was proof that pigs were among the smartest of farm animals. In addition to responding to his name, Eddie also was especially fond of Hershey chocolate bars.

Hoffman still wanted to keep Eddie's presence secret, but Dick Orr convinced him that Eddie was too good of a story not be told. Hoffman said that Eddie was his "first gentlemanly pig in 48 years in the pig business."

"It all happened in the spring," he said, "when the pig, then 7 weeks old, took to what appeared to be his deathbed after being weaned."

Hoffman said he and his wife, Fannie Maye, placed Eddie in a warm spot in the barn, nursed him like a baby, and put him on a diet of oatmeal and milk. They also began feeding him Hershey chocolate bars.

"Eddie is a smart pig and a perfect gentleman," said Hoffman. "Unlike other pigs, he never fights his way to a trough, but walks around and finds a place of his own."

Dick Orr had assigned me to do the story on Eddie, and to get further information, I sought comment from another expert, Charley Wheeler, a representative of the Chicago Producers Commission Association.

"It's the darndest thing I've seen in 50 years in the stock-yards—a pig that answers to his own name," said Wheeler. "It just goes to show you that if people would only give a pig a chance, it can be the smartest animal in the farm lot."

After we had sent the story to the *Tribune* desk by tele-graph, an editor called and said we should get a photo-graph of Eddie. He said he was sending out a good photographer, Bill Vendetta.

It was already dark when Bill got to us at the Amphitheatre, but he and I headed for a large barn west of the Amphitheatre to find Eddie. I told Bill that before going I had to get a Hershey chocolate bar for Eddie. Bill was a city-born Chicagoan who probably didn't know a whole lot about where pork chops came from, and he thought Dick and I were a little crazy with this idea of going out to find a pig, call it by name and give it a chocolate candy bar.

When Bill and I finally arrived, the large barn that housed the hogs was completely dark; we fumbled around and finally found the switch to turn on the lights. It was a large place with at least two dozen pens for carloads of hogs.

The pens were not marked by any identification, so I told Bill that the only thing we could do would be to go from pen to pen hollering "Eddie!" All the hogs in each pen had crowded up together and were peacefully snoring. The first three or four pens that we tried produced no result. Then came the fifth pen. After I had yelled, "Eddie, Eddie," a pig jumped up and came prancing over to us. I extended the chocolate candy bar and the pig took it immediately. We obviously had found Eddie.

Our story and picture of Eddie in the next morning's *Tribune* made Eddie an instant celebrity. Because of the interest, the manager of the Livestock Exposition, William E. Ogilvie, had Eddie placed in a special pen at the main entrance of the Amphitheatre so that everyone could see Eddie the Educated Pig.

We mentioned in a subsequent story that Eddie was to be given to the USO and then auctioned off to provide funds for the USO's work of serving visiting military personnel in Chicago. This story attracted the attention of the director of Brookfield Zoo, Robert Bean.

Bean called us at the Amphitheatre and said that he would like to have Eddie at Brookfield as the first inhabitant of a new section of farm animals. This led to a plan whereby Dick Orr and I, with Eddie on a leash, took Eddie in a cab one afternoon downtown to the USO headquarters in the 200 block of North Michigan Avenue. As we got out of the cab, Eddie apparently was excited and as a result had to stop for nature's call at the curb. This attracted even more attention.

Eddie was turned over to the USO for an auction. As the high bidder by prearrangement, a civic leader, Joel Goldblatt, paid the USO $1,000 for Eddie.

Goldblatt then turned Eddie over to Bean, the Brookfield Zoo director, who christened Eddie as the initial inhabitant of the zoo's barnyard section.

The last that Dick Orr and I heard about Eddie was five years later when he passed on. No one had kept a record of how many children Eddie had entertained, but he had grown so heavy from eating Hershey chocolate bars that he could hardly stand up at the end.

I was involved in another Livestock Exposition story that showed how an honest and frank answer by a 16-year-old farm girl could trigger what might well be called a miracle.

It happened in 1954, when I was once again helping Dick Orr cover the show, and he asked me to do the first edition story on the competition for the Grand Steer Championship.

Janice Hullinger, who lived on a farm near Manly, Iowa, had won the Junior Steer Competition championship with her 1,080-pound black steer. This competition was among farm girls and boys ages 12 to 21. Winning the junior championship entitled Janice to move up with her steer to the Open Beef Cattle Competition and compete for the Grand Championship.

In 55 years of the International Livestock show, however, only nine winners of the Junior Competition had won the Grand Championship in competition with adult exhibitors.

It was already something of a miracle that Janice had won the Junior Competition. She had brought her steer, an Aberdeen Angus named Shorty, straight from the farm with little or no knowledge of how to exhibit it, but with faith that Shorty was the best steer in the country.

After Janice and her steer arrived at the Amphitheatre, two strangers, Eugene Schubert, 39, and Bud McBride, 23, herdsman from Hamilton, Missouri, volunteered to help Janice groom and primp Shorty for making the best possible appearance before the judges.

For the final competition, Janice and Shorty were in the ring in the Amphitheatre with five other steer owners and their entries. A large crowd looked on as the judge went slowly from one steer to another, making his inspection. He went around slowly a second time and then a third time.

Finally, the judge stopped and slapped a steer on the rump. It was Shorty—the new Grand Champion Steer.

Janice was sobbing with joy as I rushed up to get a quick interview for my first edition story.

"As a winner, you will be getting quite a bit of money for Shorty," I said to her. "What is it that you would most like to have?"

Without hesitation, Janice replied, "Indoor plumbing. More than anything else, I wish we had indoor plumbing."

Having grown up in a farming community with only outdoor plumbing, I knew exactly how Janice felt.

My story got the top headline in the *Tribune*, and in the third paragraph, I used Janice's answer to my question: "Indoor plumbing. More than anything else, I wish we had indoor plumbing."

Among the *Tribune* readers of that story were the top executives of the Crane Company, the Chicago-based manufacturer of plumbing equipment. The result was a special offer by the Crane Company, which was disclosed six months later at a national press conference at the Hullinger farm. By chartered plane, the Crane Company brought a group of journalists and photographers to a press conference at the Hullinger farm in Iowa to show an example of how a farmhouse could be modernized.

A septic tank had been installed for the indoor plumbing. An old outdoor well with a hand pump had been replaced by a basement well with an electric motor. The Crane Company also installed two bathrooms and modernized the kitchen. The company provided the equipment and did all of the work at no cost to Janice and her family.

Needless to say, Janice and her family could hardly believe everything that had happened. Special national attention had already been given to Janice and her champion steer just after the Livestock Exposition in Chicago had closed. She and her steer were flown by chartered plane to New York City, where they appeared on the Ed Sullivan "Toast of the Town" television program. This was arranged by Gustave Allgauer, a Chicago restaurant proprietor, who had bought Shorty at auction for $16,650.

As a reporter, I have always had fun doing something that had never been done before to see if it would work.

In one instance, in April of 1959, I made the front page of the *Tribune* with something that was out of the ordinary. Here was the story that ran under my byline.

> Bill Cox, sheriff of Coles County in downstate Illinois, received a special request from a stranger.
>
> "I am writing you for help in recovering a hat I left in a restaurant while driving though Mattoon early Sunday morning on my way back from vacation," read a letter postmarked "Evanston."
>
> "I don't know the name of the restaurant, but it is on the east side of Route 45 at the north end of Mattoon. It is a good restaurant, apparently known for its large servings of wheat cakes, which a number of customers were enjoying when my wife and I and our two small children stopped there."
>
> The letter also noted the size, color and make of the hat, along with the fact that the owner's initials were stamped inside.
>
> "I am enclosing $1 as postage in the event the hat is found," the letter concluded.
>
> The writer identified himself only by name and home address. There was no indication on the letterhead or envelope of a business affiliation.
>
> The letter had been addressed merely to, "The Sheriff of Coles County, Mattoon, Ill." The address of Mattoon actually was an error, for the letter had to be forwarded to the county seat, Charleston.
>
> Four days later, the hat, packed in a sturdy box, was delivered by the postman in Evanston.
>
> There also was an envelope mailed separately. The postage for the hat came to 34 cents. The sheriff's envelope cost the usual 4 cents to send, and inside there was 62 cents in stamps as change.
>
> To this reporter—the stranger who lost and recovered his hat—Sheriff Bill Cox of Coles County was a most accommodating man.

DIARY OF SNAKE BITE DEATH

Curator Details 15-Hour Ordeal

Believed Poison Dose Wouldn't Be Fatal

That was the banner headline on the front page of the *Chicago Tribune* on October 3, 1957, for an exclusive story I had gotten.

It was one of a kind—a truly unique story. There had been stories about snakebite deaths, but probably few, if any, stories based on a diary written by a victim as he was dying.

As the *Tribune* reporter covering the Cook County Building, I got the exclusive about the snakebite diary quite by luck.

An obituary already had been published about the snakebite death of Dr. Karl P. Schmidt at the age of 67. A nationally known herpetologist, he was a curator emeritus of zoology at Chicago's Natural History Museum, better known as the Field Museum.

He had been bitten September 25 as he was examining a South African boomslang snake that had been brought to him from the Lincoln Park Zoo for identification. Dr. Schmidt had collapsed and died the next day in his home in suburban Homewood, just as he was planning to return to work.

The funeral had been held, but still pending was an investigation by the Coroner's Office, which at that time had the governmental responsibility of determining the causes of unnatural deaths. (The coroner has since been replaced by the medical examiner in Cook County.)

I had a hunch that there might be something more to the story than had been told, so I asked a clerk in the Coroner's Office if I could see the personal effects of Dr. Schmidt that were being held as possible evidence in the investigation.

That's how I found the diary. It was written in the perfect penmanship of the old school on several sheets of ruled note paper. It covered a 15-hour period from the time Dr. Schmidt boarded a suburban train at 4:30 p.m. on the day he was bitten until the next morning.

He wrote that he was afflicted with strong nausea, chills and fever, and bleeding, from the mucous membranes of the mouth. His last entry, which was written the next day, read, "Mouth and nose continuing to bleed, but not excessively."

His associates said that he apparently had made no further entries because he was up and around the next day and had notified his office that he would be returning to work.

Unattended by a physician, Dr. Schmidt went into a coma at 2 P.M. An inhalator squad was called and worked to no avail. The coroner's record gave 3:15 p.m. as the time of death "upon arrival" at Ingalls Memorial Hospital in Harvey.

In my story about the diary, I explained that, according to medical science, the boomslang snake belongs to a hemotoxic group of reptiles with venom leading to bleeding and hemorrhages. An autopsy by the coroner's physician found that Dr. Schmidt's death was caused by cerebral hemorrhages as a result of the snake's venom.

In his introduction to the diary, Dr. Schmidt said he took the snake "without thinking of any precautions, and it promptly bit me on the fleshy lateral aspect of the first joint of the left thumb."

"The mouth was widely opened, and the bite was made with the rear fangs, only the right fang entering to its full length of about 3 millimeters," he wrote. "Only one other tooth mark from the penultimate tooth appeared on the thumb when the snake was disengaged. The punctures bled freely and I sucked them vigorously."

Alan Resetar, collection manager of the Department of Zoology at the Field Museum, said the work and writings by Dr. Schmidt as a distinguished herpetologist are still studied and appreciated by today's staff at the Museum.

"One of his most important contributions is our library of rare books that he developed," said Resetar. "His work here is well known to everyone even though that was 50 years ago."

Among the untold number of news stories and articles I have written in more than 60 years of journalism in Chicago are a few stories that I can never forget.

One such story was written late in the evening of February 13, 1951. Because it was almost the deadline for the Final Edition, I wrote the story in three-paragraph takes, which I sent immediately to the editing desk.

After reading the first two takes, our managing editor, J. Loy Maloney, came over and said he liked the story and that I should write as much as I could without any regard for space.

Here is the first part of that story:

A train weighing 228 tons squealed slowly through a brightly lit but deserted tunnel last night as a trio of engineering and transportation experts pressed noses against the window of the lead car like expectant fathers.

As the train crept up to stations, members of a special crew whipped out rules to measure distances between car steps and the platform.

Once an unexpected stop was made because of a fear that the cars would not clear an overhead signal.

It was the first time a train ever had gone over the entire route of Chicago's newest subway—the Milwaukee-Dearborn Subway designed to provide Northwest Side residents a time-saving ride to and from the downtown Loop.

The new subway, built over the last 12 years at a cost $39,600,000, will be opened for regular passenger service February 25.

For the trial run, the three experts gave a decision of "very successful."

The experts were E. A. Imhoff, executive assistant to the general manager of the Chicago Transit Authority;

George DeMent, assistant chief engineer of the city's Department of Subways and Superhighways; and Walter Grimm, engineer in charge of construction for the Department of Subways and Superhighways.

Grimm explained, "You can create the best engineering plans in the world, but you never know how they will work out until the final project is tested."

I wrote a dozen more paragraphs giving details of the construction of the Dearborn Subway, which had been delayed by World War II. (Chicago's first subway, under State Street, had been placed under construction before Pearl Harbor and was completed and opened in 1943.)

On the morning of February 14, after my story on the trial run of the Milwaukee-Dearborn Subway had appeared in the *Tribune*, I received a telephone call from Grimm, one of the three experts on that trial run.

"I want to thank you very much for mentioning me this morning in the story about the Dearborn Subway," said Grimm. "It was the first time my name ever appeared in the *Tribune*.

"The best thing about it was what my daughter told me this morning. She said, 'Dad, I always knew you were very important, and now I know how important you are after reading the *Tribune* this morning.'"

Grimm's telephone call reminded me of a gross oversight I had made some years before as an inexperienced reporter in the Financial News Department of the *Tribune*.

I had taken a delightful weekend trip in October to Quincy, Illinois, on the Mississippi River, to cover the dedication of a newly developed industrial district. Industrial districts represented something new in business and industry at that time, and the project at Quincy was a good example of how a small city could develop an industrial district.

I had a feeling of self-satisfaction for having had my first byline article on an out-of-town assignment until I heard indirectly about the effect of my story in Quincy. The mayor, the president of the Chamber of Commerce, and other civic leaders were pleased with the story for, among other things, their names had been mentioned. But I had hurt the feelings of one man who was not a public official but who, as the person who had done all the work, did not get mentioned at all. It probably is not taught in journalism schools, but I learned an important principle: One should always give credit where credit is due, even though the person might not be the highest person on the totem pole.

More than anything else, I always felt that writing stories about people was by far the most satisfying part of one's work as a reporter and writer.

In 1952 our *Tribune* managing editor, J. Loy Maloney, invited members of the staff to submit stories that would be awarded a prize and given prominent play in the paper. I don't remember what the prize was, but I have kept a copy of a story I did. It brings back wonderful memories of a group of us who got together for early morning coffee and of the charming person who served us.

The story reads:

> Lil is a North Michigan Avenue waitress with a hot pot of coffee and a warm heart.
>
> She presides over her domain (the north end of a long counter) with the graciousness of a society matron, the sincerity of a lifelong friend and the genuineness of a hen clucking over chicks.
>
> Lil's coffee drinkers are an assorted lot. There are youngsters fresh from school and eager to get on in the world. Others are aged in varying degrees by years and experience.
>
> There is a variety of individuals, cares and troubles. A father worries about a son approaching draft age. Another wonders how he is going to make a down payment on a house. A young woman pines for a handsome (and perhaps wealthy) husband.

Under the spell of Lil's coffee pot, everyone seems to find common ground. Lil and her coffee pot are an invitation to a spell of good company and good conversation.

Lil is on the job from early morning until evening, six days a week, administering to her charges. They can't be described as customers, for most of them never order anything other than a dime cup of coffee. Refills are free.

The health and well-being of everyone is of special interest to Lil. She notes the bags under eyes and prescribes sleep. A hangover victim with bloodshot eyes is cautioned, "You ought to take it a little easier, baby."

A member of Lil's club becomes ill and goes to the hospital. She slips out to a flower shop. That evening she pays a visit to the hospital.

Lil bubbles with a sense of humor. A young lady accidentally dips part of her blouse into a cup of coffee. Later, Lil makes a trip to the 5 & 10-cent store. The next morning she presents her customer with a toy washing machine.

A male coffee drinker is distinguished by glowing red cheeks. Lil makes another trip to the 5 & 10. For her friend with the red cheeks, she has a toy stove—and a new nickname, Little Firepot.

Lil's charges are a pampered group. One, for instance, was fuzzy about his diet. He abhorred the thought of making a decision from a menu.

Now, at mealtime, Lil watches for this customer to leave his place of work across the street. When he arrives, his place is set and his food is on the counter. Lil has gone ahead and made up his mind for him.

Lil is one of Chicago's biggest buyers of remembrance cards. There is always a welcome-back card signed by other coffee sippers for each of her many club members on return from vacation or extended absence.

No one knows how she learns of birthdays, but several days before a birthday, Lil produces a card and requests the signatures of all of the other coffee drinkers. At times, a half-dozen such cards may be in the making.

It undoubtedly is just an unintentional human error, but it is doubtful if any of Lil's many coffee drinkers have the faintest idea when her birthday is.

Lil, who is Miss Lillian Wheedon, will be in full flush of modesty when she sees this in print.

As a reporter covering local government, I once turned up a story about a 76-year-old spinster who lived in North Tarrytown, New York, repaying Cook County for a favor that had been extended to her 48 years before, when she was a stranger in need of help in Chicago.

"Enclosed herewith is a postal money order from North Tarrytown for $200," wrote Miss Mabel Casey. "It is in payment for an operation I had in the summer of 1910 in the Cook County Hospital."

The letter contained no other information, but in a telephone conversation Miss Casey, now the operator of a rooming house, told the *Tribune:*

"I had come to Chicago all alone from New York, early in 1910, hoping to get a job as a stenographer. Jobs were not easy to get, and I had very little to go on when I needed an abdominal operation.

"They were very kind to me at County Hospital, and I was there for several weeks. Six months later I went back to New York, but I have never forgotten the kindness of those people at the hospital.

"This has always been hanging over my head, and some years ago I began laying a little money aside just to pay the hospital. They never gave me a bill for the operation.

"But I figured that in 1910 the operation and hospital care must have cost about $100. And I figured that because money was really worth more then, that the $100 of 1910 would amount to about $200 now."

Miss Casey's payment was considered so unusual that it was brought to the official attention of the County Board supervisor of the hospital, a public institution where patients pay only if they can afford to.

A half-mile stretch of Sheridan Road linking Chicago and Evanston became a personal issue for me in the spring of 1968. I like to think that the whole community benefited as a result.

Before 1968, this half-mile of Sheridan, which curves around Calvary Cemetery at the lakefront between Juneway Terrace in Chicago and South Boulevard in Evanston, was extremely dangerous. There were two 90-degree turns and no median strip to separate the four lanes of traffic—two north, two south.

Early on a Saturday afternoon in April of 1968, I was driving north towards Evanston and was making the 90-degree turn just beyond Juneway Terrace at the south end of this stretch. As I was making my turn, a driver coming south in a sports car simply missed the turn and banged into my car. Fortunately, I was driving a four-door car, and the blow was at the rear of the car, thus saving me from any injury. The car, however, had to be junked.

I was furious because it was an accident that probably would not have happened if there had been a median strip at the turn. I felt compelled to write a story about it. In researching the accident file of the *Tribune's* morgue (reference room), I found that this half-mile stretch of Sheridan Road could well qualify as the most dangerous half-mile of highway in Illinois.

In the preceding three years, there had been three deaths from automobile accidents there, and 22 accidents in the last two years had occurred at the southeast corner of the cemetery, where I had been hit.

Altogether, there had been 160 accidents in the last three years.

I wrote a story telling about this hazardous half-mile of Sheridan Road for "use at any time" in the *Tribune*. Editors on duty on Sunday often are hard up for good stories, so my story about Sheridan Road ended up on the front page of a Monday morning issue. The story caught the attention of the Illinois public works director, Francis Lorenz, who was serving under Governor Otto Kerner. I was well acquainted with both of them, having known Governor Kerner when he was county judge and Lorenz when he was Cook County treasurer.

That Monday morning, I received a telephone call from Lorenz.

"Tom, that was an interesting story this morning," he said. "It just happens that we have some extra public works money on hand, and we will immediately make the improvement of Sheridan Road at Calvary Cemetery a special project."

A month or so later, Lorenz made public the plan for the Sheridan Road improvement. As an immediate measure, he ordered a reduction in the speed limit, hoping to decrease the accident risk.

"We are not intending to do a piecemeal or patchwork job here," Lorenz announced. "We plan to make a major improvement that will eliminate the hazards of this dangerous portion of Sheridan Road."

The plan included the construction of a median strip; curbs and gutters to define clearly the route of travel; reconstruction of the two curves near the lakefront; removal of large trees that had been often hit by vehicles; use of skid-resistant pavement material; and the channeling of traffic at the approach of the turn at the southeast corner of the cemetery, with a painted center line being replaced by a raised rumbler driving strip.

Wayne Anderson, city manager of Evanston, said the city also had plans to improve its portion of this stretch of Sheridan with new modern highway lights and better drainage.

Later, Anderson telephoned me and said, "You know, Tom, we have a number of other needed projects in Evanston we would like to have you help us with."

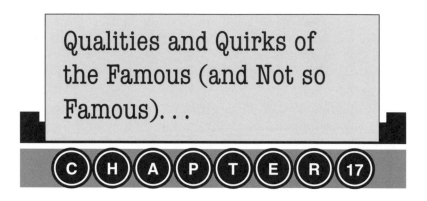

Qualities and Quirks of the Famous (and Not so Famous)...

CHAPTER 17

For more than 10 years, I had the pleasure of covering the monthly meetings of the board of trustees of the University of Illinois. Initially, I drew this assignment because of a controversy concerning the site for a new U. of I. campus in Chicago to replace the use of Navy Pier as a post-World War II campus. Locating the Chicago campus was a problem of city planning. I had covered city planning as a regular assignment for many years, and I was automatically assigned to the campus planning problem.

For several years I covered a dispute that broke out when the site at Harrison and Halsted streets on the Near West Side was selected for the new U. of I. campus. A citizens' group charged that Mayor Richard J. Daley's administration had double-crossed the community on grounds that an initial 50 acres had been earmarked exclusively for new homes.

The fight, which was carried to the Illinois and United States Supreme Courts, was spearheaded by the Harrison-Halsted Community Group, Inc., led by Mrs. Florence Scala, 45, a housewife, and Miss Jessie Binford, 86, a veteran social worker and one-time associate of Jane Addams, the founder of Hull House.

For their monthly meetings, the U. of I. trustees alternated between Chicago and the U. of I. campus in Urbana.

Among his many beats for the Chicago Tribune, *Tom Buck covered the City Plan Commission. He is shown here with Ira Bach, then City Plan Commissioner and architect of many changes in the Chicago landscape.*

For me, the meetings in Urbana were the most enjoyable because they gave me an opportunity to ride one of the last great railroad passenger trains—the Panama Limited of the Illinois Central. The Urbana meetings were held on Wednesday morning, so I took the Panama Limited leaving Chicago at 5 P.M. on Tuesday.

The train took a little over two hours to get to Urbana, just enough time for me to enjoy a gourmet dinner in the dining car.

One of the members of the U. of I. board was Wayne Johnston, president of the Illinois Central. As the railroad's president, he traveled in the Presidential Car, which consisted of a lounge at the rear, a spacious dining room, and a bedroom with an adjoining bath. Occasionally, Johnston would invite two of us reporters along with several trustees to ride with him in the Presidential Car for the return to Chicago late Wednesday afternoon. It was always a memorable occasion.

Johnston did not like alcoholic beverages but treated us as his guests to one cocktail in the lounge at the start of the return trip. We then moved to the dining room.

The meal, which took more than an hour and a half, would have pleased the most critical of gourmets. After soup and salad, there was a fish dish, and then meat, usually a roast. There would be a choice of several desserts.

On one occasion, Johnston was dieting. Demonstrating the utmost of self-discipline, Johnston sat with a small can of the diet drink Metracal on his serving plate as the rest of us enjoyed the dinner.

As a special assignment in Urbana, I covered the opening session on March 6, 1968, of the centennial celebration of the founding of the university.

The main guest speaker was Dr. Kingman Brewster, then president of Yale University, who shocked students and faculty members with a prediction of what university life would be like 100 years in the future.

"I foresee an American society in 2068 so affluent that no one will voluntarily do many of the unpleasant tasks of our society," said Dr. Brewster.

"By that time, we would hope, there will be no need for compulsory military service. Instead, a useful purpose could be served by requiring undergraduate students to perform such tasks as garbage collection as part of their learning process."

He explained that university undergraduates would be available for such duties because most note-taking classroom sessions would be eliminated by self-learning through the use of videotapes and computers.

The "garbage man draft" for undergraduates, Dr. Brewster explained, would be a highlight of what he foresaw as a sweeping revolution in education in the coming century. He explained that in the future, videotape and computers not only would eliminate much classroom instruction, but also would make possible continuing education for all interested adults seeking "tombstone degrees."

He explained further that such "tombstone degrees" would be awarded late in the life of students, who would continue their schooling by selecting educational television courses. In addition to selecting their own educational programs, the adult students could reach central computers by telephone to seek additional information.

He said that while such electronic knowledge already was available in 1968, a massive production effort would be needed to make such equipment adaptable for "higher education in the home."

Whether the Internet is meeting Dr. Brewster's prediction or not is arguable, but as yet there is little movement toward utilizing students as garbage collectors.

Dr. Brewster also predicted that universities of the future would be financed for the most part by federal government "educare" programs. He emphasized, however, that extensive federal aid to education should not be made unless universities maintain their own control over curricula. Such federal aid, he added, "should be extended to private as well as to public universities."

During my many years as a newspaper reporter, I felt sorry for my friends who were confined to the office in editing jobs. Besides witnessing events, we reporters had the pleasure of getting to know many different types of people.

For instance, the death of W. Clement Stone on September 3, 2002, reminded me of a very unusual incident that had occurred many years before.

Stone, who died at the age of 100, was a self-made multimillionaire who had founded the Combined Insurance Company of America and who generously shared his wealth through large bequests for public purposes, particularly in the field of education.

I knew of Stone mostly because a good friend of mine, Lou Fink, was one of his public relations advisors. As a ghost writer, I helped Fink from time to time with his preparation of news releases and other material for Stone.

The Stones were very family-oriented. When I was a cubmaster in Evanston, one of Stone's grandsons, Michael Stone, was in our troop. When we had our annual Cub Scout Blue and Gold Banquet, Michael's father, W. Clement Stone, Jr., who was working in London, flew in solely to enjoy our spaghetti dinner with Michael and his Cub Scout friends.

In 1969, Illinois Governor Richard Ogilvie appointed the senior Stone to fill a vacancy on the board of trustees of the University of Illinois. The appointment was unusual because trustees usually had been alumni of the U. of I., and Stone was not.

He missed his first three meetings due to prior commitments but announced that he would be able to attend the December meeting in Urbana.

On Tuesday evening before the meeting, I had just arrived at the Union Building, where I usually stayed, when the secretary of the board came up to me and said that the trustees would like to see me. They were holding a closed pre-board meeting that evening.

Howard Clement, the board president, said that the board had been told that I was acquainted with Stone and that they would appreciate my telling them about him.

I concluded my description of Stone with this comment: "Don't be surprised at what he might do."

The next morning the board meeting had been under-way for more than an hour before Stone arrived. He apol-ogized, explaining that he had had dinner the night before with President Nixon at the White House. (Stone had been a contributor of $2 million to Nixon's presidential campaign.)

As Stone joined the meeting, the board's African-American member, Theodore Jones, of Chicago, was telling about a need for more tuition waivers to help more minor-ity students enroll in the U. of I. College of Law in Urbana. Jones said there were only 20 African-American students out of a total enrollment of more than 500 law students.

At that point, Stone interrupted Jones by saying, "This sounds like a question of money."

Stone then added, "I would personally like to finance a program for as many black students or underprivileged students to attend the College of Law as can be brought here next fall."

A staff member indicated that the number might be as great as 100 or more.

Obviously taken back by Stone's offer, one trustee asked, "Can we take money like this?"

Dr. David Dodds Henry, the U. of I. president, said, "I don't know why not."

Stone then asked the secretary of the board to make cer-tain that his program was entered into the minutes so that it could become official. Stone also explained that his financial plan was similar to a program of the Nixon Administration.

"The Nixon Administration is being successful in a new approach whereby private industry is helping to pay for many programs that are carried out in conjunction with government," he said.

"There are many cases where the private sector can well afford to pay for public programs in addition to the taxes they pay. For such programs, it often takes no more than men with the means and the ability to get such programs off the ground."

Tom Buck (right) also covered meetings of the University of Illinois trustees. He is shown here with U. of I. President David Dodds Henry.

In Chicago, Stone assigned a young attorney, Gary H. Rieman, to develop an ongoing procedure for providing the financial aid for minority law students , partly through the W. Clement and Jessie V. Stone Foundation.

Quite by coincidence 33 years later, I met Rieman at the memorial service for Mr. Stone, and I asked him what had happened with the financial aid program.

As a first step, he said, Chicago's five largest banks were contacted, and they readily agreed to participate by providing guaranteed student loans. With this help, Rieman said that the initial plan consisted of two parts totaling $1.5 million a year in aid for the minority students in the U. of I. College of Law. Of that total, he said, $500,000 consisted of direct grants by the Stone Foundation and $1 million in guaranteed loans by the banks.

Subsequently, he said, the state government came into the program by helping with the hard-to-collect loans.

Rieman, who had become director of the Illinois Student Assistance Commission, explained that a major objective has been to get the participation of other philanthropists, in addition to the grants by the Stone Foundation, in the grant phase of the program.

The success by the U. of I. College of Law in recruiting minority and underprivileged students, Rieman said, was shown in the latest enrollment figures for the year 2002. Of a total of 642 law students, 10 percent were African-American, 9 percent Asian and 9 percent Hispanic. There were two students of Native American descent.

If you think about it, it is often strange how we associate things to remember them.

For instance, take the name of Don Maxwell, who was one of the *Tribune's* top editors.

I still associate his name with fried chicken—and a story I have verified as true.

Maxwell, an avid Hoosier from Greencastle, Indiana, never ceased extolling the hospitality of Indiana and the superiority of its fried chicken. No one anywhere in the world could fry chicken like the Hoosier housewives, he contended.

He once seized a rare opportunity to prove it.

Late in the summer of 1940 Maxwell took an editorial team by station wagon to Elwood, Indiana, the hometown of Wendell Willkie, who was scheduled to make a formal acceptance of the Republican nomination for the presidency.

With Maxwell to cover the event were two reporters, Percy Wood and Clay Gowran; a telegrapher, John Mooney; and Maxwell's assistant and driver, John Schultz.

On the way back to Chicago, Maxwell again began expounding about Hoosier hospitality and fried chicken,

"Why, I bet we could stop almost any place, and they would make us welcome," he was quoted as saying.

A minute or so later, as they approached a lane to a farmhouse, Maxwell told Schultz, "Let's turn in here."

The farm wife responded to his knock on the front door.

"Madam, we are so sorry to bother you," Maxwell said, "but we are a group of newspapermen from Chicago, and we are hot and tired and hungry, and we wonder if it would be too much to ask you to fix us a fried chicken dinner."

"Well, I guess I could if you could wait about 45 minutes," she replied.

"Meanwhile, you could make yourselves at home here on the front porch," she said, pointing to the swing and chairs.

From all reports, it was a superb dinner, complete with the fried chicken, mashed potatoes and gravy, green beans and salad, topped off with apple pie.

"Why, I wouldn't think of taking a cent," she told Maxwell, as they were about to leave.

But Schultz reported that he was certain that Maxwell had put a generous offering under his plate.

It seems to me that today's newspapers, as well as other media, are making some mistakes by not covering certain things that years ago made headlines.

The criminal courts are being covered, but little or no attention seems to be paid to the civil courts, including Probate Court, which handles the certification of wills and estates.

In Probate Court there are always at least two good stories about interesting estates—one when the will is filed and a second when the inventory or listing of assets is filed. Usually the biggest news from Probate Court pertains to the wills in which significant bequests are made to charitable and public organizations, such as The Salvation Army, the Red Cross and universities.

In large estates, the inventories are always interesting with regard to the size of the estates and the types of assets and investments.

In one instance, I was involved in the handling of an estate of a long-time *Tribune* editorial employee who, for one reason or another, was believed to have been living near the poverty level.

Charles Collins, who died at the age of 83, was kept on the staff because the managing editor thought he needed financial help. Collins, who lived alone in an apartment in Evanston, had been a Chicago newspaperman for 60 years, 33 of which he had spent with the *Tribune*.

He was a very learned man who had graduated from the University of Chicago, where he was a founder of *The Daily Maroon* newspaper. He had written three books and two plays, was a highly recognized drama critic, reviewed books, and in his later years edited "A Line O'Type or Two," a popular editorial page column of prose, poetry and humor.

He had joined the Cliff Dwellers in 1912, five years after that club was founded, and was a founding member of the Tavern Club. The Chicago Press Veterans honored him as Press Veteran of the Year in 1951.

He was known as a charming, Dickens-like bachelor of little financial means. He reportedly was given free evening dinners at the Tavern Club, and Don Maxwell, the *Tribune* managing editor, was said to have kept him on the staff out of the goodness of his heart.

In the County Building pressroom, I received a telephone call one day from an attorney, William Boyden, who said he had a special request to make concerning Mr. Collins' estate.

"I am handling the estate," said Boyden, "and I would like to have you find out if the *Tribune* could suppress the news about the estate. Also, I hope you could get your fellow reporters in the pressroom to keep the story out of the other papers.

"Believe it or not, Collins left an estate of more than $1 million. His only heir is a niece, who kept close tabs on him by having him over every Sunday for a family dinner.

"The niece and her husband have one child, a 6-year-old daughter. The niece had no idea that Collins had an estate like this, and she is very worried that if this news gets out, her daughter might be kidnapped. She is very emotional about this, and she says that this must be kept a secret."

I asked Boyden how Collins, on a newspaperman's pay, was able to accumulate an estate of more than $1 million.

"He apparently watched every penny," said Boyden. "But more than that, he invested in good stocks over many years and kept reinvesting the dividends. He bought stock in only five companies—General Motors, AT&T, DuPont, General Electric and Commonwealth Edison."

When I told Maxwell about the estate, he almost bit his cigar in two.

"I thought he didn't have a dime," said Maxwell. "That's why I kept him on here at the *Tribune.*"

The *Tribune* and the other papers agreed not to print anything about the estate.

At the request of the niece, I spent the next Saturday with her helping to go through the books in Collins' apartment. We shook out all of his books of recent years because he had developed a habit of using dividend checks for bookmarks. We recovered quite a number of checks.

Besides working full-time for the *Tribune,* I did a considerable amount of freelance work over the years. I was always careful not to let this extra work interfere with my *Tribune* assignments or place me in a conflict-of-interest dilemma.

Some of the work was for trade or industry publications. I wrote a weekly column, which required making only three telephone calls, about the retailing of photographic equipment. Under the pen name of F. Meyer, I wrote articles about ice cream and candy for a confectionery industry magazine.

Quite often, I wrote major articles on local government and industry for a magazine published by the Chicago Association of Commerce and Industry. I didn't go to work for the *Tribune* until 10 a.m., so I did much of my extra writing early in the morning. A friend of mine let me use his office in the Loop. To meet deadlines, I would go downtown very early in the morning on elevated trains from our home in Evanston. Beginning at 6 a.m., I could get a lot of writing done in four hours in my friend's office before checking in with the *Tribune* at 10 o'clock.

In addition to monthly magazine articles, I also did other writing for the Association of Commerce and Industry. I was especially busy as a freelance writer in 1959 when the Commerce Association sponsored an International Trade Show at Navy Pier in connection with the opening of the St. Lawrence Seaway and a visit to Chicago by Queen Elizabeth II of England. Besides news releases, I wrote speeches for various officers of the Commerce Association.

One year I was given the unusual assignment of writing five speeches for the annual meeting of the Commerce Association. The speeches, each for five minutes, were to be given by the current Association president and four previous presidents. To prepare the speeches, I interviewed all five of the speakers.

At the annual meeting luncheon, I happened to be at the press table as an observer; and as the ghost speechwriter, I took a special pleasure in commenting to the working reporters that I thought the "speeches were especially well-written." None of the reporters, of course, had any idea that I had written them.

A week later, Ruth and I happened to have two good friends, Errett Graham and his wife, Edith, over to our house for dinner. Errett was a very fine independent attorney who had a mind of his own. He was a liberal Democrat who left no doubt about his political beliefs. The *Tribune*, with its conservative Republican editorials, was not for him.

It was "the principle of the thing" that was foremost in Errett's mind. As his own attorney, he once took a $5 traffic ticket all the way to the Illinois Supreme Court to win the case on grounds that due process of law had not been followed in the issuance of the ticket. A principle had been violated, he contended successfully.

At the dinner at our house, Errett said he had some news to report.

Somewhat in conflict with his better judgment, Errett said, he had finally joined the Chicago Association of Commerce and Industry. He did not believe in many of the conservative policies the Association stood for, but he thought it would be better for his law practice if he were to join and make contacts with possible clients.

I remember Errett saying something very much like this:

"I attended the annual meeting of the Association last week and it was very plain to me that the Association and I have very little, if anything, in common.

"Those speeches by the president and the former presidents sounded like a replay of a lot of Republican propaganda. I didn't agree with any of it, but it was very clever writing. They must have paid a lot of money to get those speeches written by some high-powered public relations firm."

At that point, my wife, Ruth, burst out laughing. She simply couldn't restrain herself.

"What's the matter with you?" asked Errett.

Ruth replied, "I'm very sorry, Errett. But I couldn't help myself. You probably can't believe this, but those speeches were written on that countertop in our kitchen. Tom does freelance work for the Association, and he was the ghostwriter for the annual meeting. He wrote all of those speeches."

Errett was lost for words, but he finally managed to mumble some kind of an apology.

There Is Life After Newspaper Reporting

Public Relations for the CTA...

CHAPTER 18

When I was hired by the *Tribune* in September of 1940, I thought I would be a *Tribune* reporter and writer for the rest of my life. Thirty-three years later, however, I did not feel quite the same.

It seemed that much of the fun was gone.

It had been like a good team that had grown old. Most of the players were still around, but gone were nearly all of the old coaches—the editors who provided direct contact and guidance for the reporters. Clayton Kirkpatrick, a good friend, was still there, but he had moved up to the top position, editor of the *Tribune*, where he had little daily contact with reporters.

Long gone was J. Loy Maloney, my first managing editor; and no longer there were Don Maxwell, the city editor who moved up to top editor, and assignment editors Tom Furlong, Phil Hampson, Stanley Armstrong and Harold Murray.

In most instances, the replacements were fine, I'm sure; but they didn't seem the same to me. I had been used to working closely with editors, but with the new managing editor I could not establish any relationship whatsoever. My memos to him about possible stories went unanswered.

I had had a standing offer from the Chicago Transit Authority for nearly 10 years, since the retirement of Harry Polland, the public relations director who had been with the CTA since it began operating in 1947. The job had been offered to me originally by the CTA's first general manager, Walter J. McCarter.

Because the public relations director was the official spokesman for the CTA, it was considered an important position; and even the president of the main CTA union, Daniel McNamara, had encouraged me to take the job.

So, having become somewhat disenchanted with the *Tribune*, I turned to the Chicago Transit Authority in August of 1973. I was hired by the two top CTA officials, Milton Pikarsky, the chairman, and Thomas B. O'Connor, the general manager.

My job at the CTA, which had the title of public affairs manager, took in a wide range of communication relationships. Besides newspapers, we developed close connections with radio and television stations.

We also handled CTA advertising, publications and customer service, which involved mostly complaints and commendations. We had a major role in the staging of special events. For CTA board meetings, we prepared a presentation of information of current happenings on the CTA.

Through our press releases, we also developed closer relationships with the minority communities in Chicago. We worked closely with the African-American community in various ways, such as taking part in the annual Bud Billiken Parade and promoting the DuSable Museum as a major stop on our Culture Bus route.

In addition to the African-American community, we paid special attention to the Hispanic and Asian community media. One of our secretaries, Elda Leal, who was a leader in the Mexican-American community, took on additional duties as a community representative and a transla-

Promotional activities, such as this display of T-shirts advertising routes and maps, were a big part of Tom Buck's activity at the Chicago Transit Authority.

tor of press releases into Spanish for the Hispanic newspapers. Similarly, another of our staff members, Larry Paek, a Korean-American, translated our press releases into Korean and became our representative with the Asian community.

With more than 22 employees, our Public Affairs Department was so busy with different activities that the administration of the department itself was a big job. Fortunately, we had an excellent experienced staff executive, Bill Baxa, as deputy manager, to handle much of the administrative work.

In addition to CTA matters, I also became very much involved in the promotion of new state legislation to create the Regional Transportation Authority as an overall agency in the Chicago area for the CTA, the commuter railroads and suburban buses. Pikarsky, our CTA chairman, was very active in the promotion of RTA as Mayor Richard J. Daley's main representative, and I was the chief speechwriter in that effort.

By far the most interesting part of my work as CTA public affairs manager was my contact with radio and television stations. The effectiveness of television particularly was unbelievable in comparison with newspapers and other print media. If one appeared only a minute or two on an evening TV news show, one would be greeted on the street the next day by all types of people, most of whom were complete strangers.

"Oh, I saw you on TV last night," a waitress would say.

I was with the CTA from September of 1973 until March of 1980, and during those seven years there were a number of accidents on the elevated transit system. These occurred just before a new electronic safety system was installed on the elevated right-of-way which, for the first time, would automatically prevent trains from running into each other. From the very start, the CTA subways under State and Dearborn streets had safety signal systems, but only short sections of the elevated right-of-way had had such protection.

When accidents occurred, our Public Affairs Department practiced what we called "crisis management public relations." In such emergencies, there can be only one spokesman, and I usually filled that duty, fielding questions from the newspapers, and radio and TV stations.

Besides the designation of one person as the sole spokesman, another cardinal rule in crisis management public relations is to be very careful about information that is given out. In all cases, the spokesman is restricted to giving out only information that is a proven fact at that time. False information not only is wrong from the standpoint of ethics, but it also can have disastrous results.

The main questions after an accident always were, "What caused the accident?" and "Were any of the operating employees responsible?" Under no circumstances could the spokesman answer those questions, inasmuch as the answers could be determined only by a thorough investigation that was carried out by the National Transportation Board.

The worst rapid transit accident during my seven years with the CTA occurred during the late-afternoon rush hour on February 4, 1977, when four elevated cars fell off the tracks at Wabash Avenue and Lake Street. Eleven riders were killed and 193 were injured.

I happened to be out of the city, so the CTA spokesman for the accident was one of my assistants, Donald Yabush. He told me that he had no trouble handling the situation because he had stuck closely to our principle of giving out only known information and refraining from doing any guessing or speculating.

Aside from accidents, one of the worst crises in the CTA's history occurred during January and early February of 1979 when the Chicago area was virtually paralyzed by huge snowstorms.

The CTA service, both bus and rapid transit, was hard hit, all of which subsequently affected an upcoming election in which Mayor Michael Bilandic was defeated by Jane Byrne in the contest to be the Democratic candidate.

At the height of the storm, fewer than one-third of the CTA's fleet of elevated-subway cars could be operated. Someone apparently had given Mayor Bilandic incorrect information because at a City Hall press conference Bilandic said he had been informed that the rapid transit service would be virtually back to normal the next day. That could not possibly have happened.

Another CTA mistake in dealing with the snowstorm had a serious backlash against Mayor Bilandic. It was a CTA operation decision that was well-intended but badly managed.

A dangerous condition had developed on several major rapid transit lines which extended from outlying areas to downtown Chicago. With the bus service being so poor, unusually large numbers of people flocked to the rapid transit stations. The trains became immediately filled at the outlying stations, and as they moved downtown there was no room for anyone to get on at the inner-city stops. There was a serious danger of people being hurt as the crowds tried to force their way onto the inbound trains.

Without any advanced notice to our Public Affairs Office, there was a sudden change in CTA operations by which the inbound rapid transit trains did not stop at any of the inner-stations after leaving the stations in the outlying communities and suburbs. It was assumed that riders in the inner part of the city could get by with the bus service, even though it was not functioning well either.

This sudden change in the CTA rapid transit operations was seized upon by politicians in the African-American community as an example of how the low-income families in the inner-city were being discriminated against.

It was a bad situation that could possibly have been improved by more advanced notice together with the operation of special trains for riders in the inner-city. As it happened, it probably cost Mayor Bilandic his job.

In our day-to-day public relations efforts, we kept in mind particularly the effectiveness of both radio and TV. For service changes, which usually became effective on Mondays, we used radio extensively. In addition to putting out an advanced release, we also repeated the release several times on Saturday and Sunday so that the various shifts of news writers at the radio stations could use the notice about Monday's service change.

To distribute these frequent news releases over the weekend, we used the public relations services which were then provided by the City News Bureau.

For television, we went out of our way to plan photo opportunities that would attract the TV camera crews and reporters. If we could obtain one or two minutes of free time on the TV stations, that would be equivalent to many

Letting his hair grow to fit the role, Tom Buck was a key actor in a CTA Benjamin Franklin promotion during the national bicentennial year.

thousands of dollars that we would otherwise be paying for commercial advertising.

Our most unusual CTA event, especially for TV coverage, occurred during the frigid hours very early on Sunday morning, December 4, 1977. It was really an event sponsored by the Public Works Department of Chicago, with Marshall Suloway as public works commissioner.

It had never happened before, and it probably will never happen again. And chances are Chicago was the only place where it could have happened. The event was moving a heavy house over the elevated tracks.

It was Chicago's oldest house—a two-story frame building with a rough-hewn oak framework that had been built in 1836, a year before Chicago was incorporated as a city. Historians referred to it as the Widow Clarke's House.

The structure, weighing 120 tons, was moved over the "El" at 44th Street on the south rapid transit route. This was the hardest maneuver in a special project of moving the old house from 4526 Wabash to 1827 Indiana Avenue, where it is now a feature of the Prairie Avenue Landmark District.

In the week before the move, by means of hydraulic jacking equipment, the house was placed on a cribbing tower on the west side of the "El" structure at a height of 27 feet, well above the track level. A similar cribbing tower was erected on the east side. When the electric power was turned off on the elevated right-of-way, two large I-beams were laid on top of the tracks from the cribbing tower on one side to the tower on the other. The house, sitting on dollies, was pulled across by means of a winch mounted on a tractor on the east side of the "El" structure, with a holdback cable and winch on the west side.

The day before, Arne Jarnholm, project manager of a machinery moving company, showed a sense of humor as well as engineering confidence when asked about the prospects of getting the house over the "El" without mishap.

"Oh, I'm sure we will make it all right," said Jarnholm. "But if we don't, there will be the biggest pile of kindling on the tracks you ever saw."

The actual move of the house over the tracks took one hour and 10 minutes, and occurred between 2:40 and 3:50 A.M. During the next three days, the hydraulic jacking equipment was used to lower the house to street level on the east side of the "El."

During my service as CTA public affairs manager, our biggest triumph was the creation of special "culture bus service" on Sundays and holidays during the summer and early fall.

For several years, I had been trying to get the CTA management to authorize a culture bus service but had been turned down because of the cost involved. I picked up the idea from New York City and Philadelphia, which were having a lot of success with culture buses.

With the CTA general manager, however, I could make no headway against the opposition, which was based on the contention that a culture bus service could not pay for itself and that it would be too much of a luxury for the CTA. I had really given up on the idea when an unexpected breakthrough took place about the first of May in 1977. Two important visitors appeared unannounced at my CTA office.

One was Heather Morgan, director of cultural affairs for the City of Chicago.

That spring we had a new Chicago mayor, Michael Bilandic, who was elected by the City Council after the death of Mayor Richard J. Daley. Heather Morgan and Mayor Bilandic were engaged to be married.

With Miss Morgan was a representative of a museum committee, Victor J. Danilov, director and later president of the Museum of Science and Industry.

They had a suggestion: It would be nice if the CTA could provide special culture buses on Sundays and holidays to get people to and from the museum and other similar points of interest.

I explained that my office had had this idea in mind for several years but that we were unable to get the general manager to approve it because of the cost.

However, I assured Miss Morgan and Mr. Danilov that I would try again and that if we were lucky, we might be able to start the service on Memorial Day, in about three weeks.

As public affairs manager, I was accountable separately to two superiors: the chairman of the CTA Board and the general manager. Our CTA chairman was James J. McDonough, who formerly was Chicago's commissioner of streets and sanitation, and who was very astute politically.

After Miss Morgan and Danilov left, I immediately telephoned McDonough about their visit and their suggestion for a culture bus service. Without any hesitation, McDonough responded:

"What the future wife of the mayor of Chicago wants, she will get. Let's get it started as soon as possible."

The CTA general manager, George Krambles, who previously had opposed the idea, now gave the culture bus his full support and, as a result, we had it running by Memorial Day.

The buses operated on Sundays and holidays between 11 A.M. and 5 P.M., running every 10 minutes to and from the Art Institute on Michigan Avenue at Adams Street. One of the main features was that riders could use "super transfers" so they could get on and off the buses at various points of interest without paying additional fares.

At first we had only one route, which went south, serving the Field Museum and other museums in that area, and then went farther south to the Museum of Science and Industry and other points of interest in Hyde Park. Later we added a north route running as far north as Lincoln Park, and then a west route serving several important ethnic museums and other points of interest on the West Side.

In the early years of the culture bus service, we had a wonderful CTA employee, Eileen Neurather, who served as the hostess and helped people on and off the buses at the Art Institute.

After Miss Morgan and Mayor Bilandic were married, the mayor asked us to run a special culture bus trip on a weekday for the commissioners and other top officials of the city government.

Another strong supporter of this CTA bus service was Ernie Banks, the former Chicago Cubs baseball player, who was a member of the CTA Board. One Sunday the Chicago Cubs had scheduled a special game involving the team's old-timers, and Ernie took that as an opportunity to have the old-time Chicago Cubs ride the culture bus before game time.

One of the unusual features of the culture buses was the commentary giving historical references and other information about the route. At first we used members of our public affairs department as commentators, but then we invited volunteers to do this work, giving them free monthly passes on the CTA as an honorarium.

The scripts for the commentaries on the three culture bus routes could well be considered as classics of Chicago literature. They were written by an able CTA public affairs staff member, Jeff Stern, who for many years served as the culture bus coordinator.

Jeff's scripts were very interesting. For instance, the script on the south route told how Charles Walgreen founded the first Walgreen drugstore in 1901 on Cottage Grove Avenue at the intersection with Bowen Street at 4100 south. His wife, Myrtle, began bringing sandwiches at noon for Walgreen and his staff, the sandwiches being so good that they were requested by customers who happened to be in the store. As a result, Mrs. Walgreen started a lunch service that for many years was a highlight of the Walgreen drugstores.

"Usually," Stern said, "about 15 volunteer commentators were required for a Sunday or holiday operation."

One of the early volunteers was a student, Michael Shiffer, who now is vice president of planning for the CTA. Another early commentator was a blind CTA employee, Steve Hastalis, who memorized his script and for whom the bus driver whispered cues about the location of the bus.

Hastalis, who works in the CTA customer service department, is a very unusual transportation buff. Although he is blind, he has traveled to all of the major cities in the United States with public transportation systems and has made audio tape recordings of the operation of trains and buses.

The culture bus service proved highly successful from the very start. In the first month, we ran a commercial on television about the service. Before the commercial, we were carrying approximately 1,000 people each Sunday on the culture buses. After the commercial had appeared on television for a week, the ridership jumped to more than 4,000.

"We can't be that successful," said Krambles, the general manager, "because we don't have enough spare buses to handle crowds like that."

So we never ran any more TV commercials.

The culture bus service was discontinued by the CTA in 1991 after 14 years of success.

"It was cancelled because it was felt that it was unfair to have a public operation in competition with several private tourist bus routes which had sprung up in the meantime," said Stern, the coordinator of the service and author of the commentaries.

Lost and found items—the various things left behind on buses and elevated-subway trains—are the subject of a continuing story of the Chicago Transit Authority. As a reporter, I wrote my first stories about this subject in the 1950s when CTA riders were leaving behind 6,000 to 9,000 items a month. Daily logs of lost items were kept at 16 bus depots and 7 "El" terminals.

One of my stories in the 1950s listed these items:

A wig that was reclaimed the next day by a musician.

Three fried chicken box lunches, reportedly eaten by the bus driver and his colleagues. (Perishables were not held for claimants.)

Several Christmas shopping bags with bottles of whiskey. In each instance, the bottles appeared to have been sampled, but the owners reclaimed them a few days later.

One pair of bedsprings on an "El" train. It was reported that some families may move to a different apartment in the early morning hours by having each family member carry a piece of furniture onto a CTA vehicle.

A woman's purse containing a package of chewing tobacco, a box of snuff and a straight-edge razor.

An automobile axle and transmission, found on the rear seat of a streetcar.

A full-size bicycle, also found on a streetcar.

A frozen chicken, chocolate layer cake, woman's used girdle, bathroom toilet seat cover, bow and arrow, table model radio and a fire extinguisher.

The most frequently left items were clothing, umbrellas and luggage.

Except for perishables, lost and found items were held for 30 days, although expensive articles might be held for six months to a year. If an article is not claimed, it is given to the finder, whether a passenger or a CTA employee.

There was the man who was en route to a banquet on a CTA North Avenue bus who had a coughing spell, which caused his false teeth to slip out. As he was about to get off the bus, he discovered his loss and asked the driver to wait a minute or so for him to look around for his teeth. He found a set and went on his way to the banquet.

The next day, however, he went to the North Avenue bus garage to report that he had claimed the wrong set of teeth. Fortunately, he found his right teeth in the collection of lost-and-found items; and as he departed he said, "Tell the gentleman who lost the other teeth that his set chewed a good steak dinner last night."

At the Grand Avenue stop on the Milwaukee-Dearborn subway, a CTA employee found a snake in a box. The snake was placed in the custody of the Anti-Cruelty Society, but no one ever showed up to claim it.

My last paragraph of that story was about two large, new leather suitcases left on a Lake Street elevated train. On the 32nd day after they were found, a man claimed the suitcases, explaining that he had just finished serving 30 days in the County Jail.

Shortly after I became the CTA public affairs manager in 1973, I received a telephone call from a prestigious jewelry company in downtown Chicago.

The company president asked for help in recovering a brown paper bag with $16,000 worth of uncut diamonds believed to have been left behind on a bus. It was explained that the bag of diamonds had been picked up at the U.S. Customs Office on the Near West Side by a deliveryman who had placed the bag on the floor of the bus and then had forgotten about it until he was back in the office.

With the help of the CTA bus operating office, we were able to telephone the bus driver and recover the diamonds, which were still in the bag on the floor of the bus.

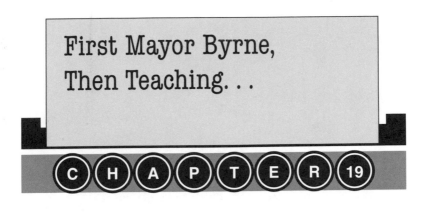

First Mayor Byrne,
Then Teaching. . .

C H A P T E R 19

The first time I met Mayor Jane Byrne was on the telephone.

It was early in her term when I was still at the CTA as public affairs manager. Her daughter, Kathy, had gone to work in our office as a reporter and writer after graduating from college. Although she had never worked before as a journalist, Kathy was an excellent writer, and she did her assignments so quickly and effectively that I had a hard time keeping her busy.

Out of a clear sky one morning came the telephone call from Mayor Byrne.

"Tom," said the mayor, "don't get excited about this, but I am going to assign a policeman as a bodyguard for Kathy.

"We have been getting a lot of threatening telephone calls, and while we're not too worried, we think it would be well to have a bodyguard for her just as a precaution."

With the policeman as Kathy's bodyguard, our office became the best protected part of the CTA headquarters in the Merchandise Mart. After a few months, we were sorry to lose Kathy when she decided to move on to try other things and eventually become a lawyer.

After that telephone call, I had no further contact with Mayor Byrne until two years later.

Tom Buck served former Chicago Mayor Jane Byrne as press secretary.

It was a brisk December day in 1981 when I ran into the mayor's husband, Jay McMullen, at the corner of Madison and Clark Streets. Jay, who had covered City Hall for the *Daily News*, had been a good friend of mine for many years.

"What are you doing these days, Tom?" he asked, knowing that I had retired from the CTA.

"Not much," I replied.

"We would like you to give us some help in the mayor's office," said Jay. "You could start right away."

I explained that Ruth and I were planning to go away for a vacation and that we wouldn't be back until after the first of the year.

"Okay, come over and see me as soon as you're back," he said.

When we returned from our trip I received a telephone call from a friend who said he had read in a newspaper gossip column that I had joined the mayor's staff. Jay had lost no time in getting the word out.

I went to Jay's office in City Hall to learn what I was to do.

"Come on, we have to see the mayor," said Jay, without any explanation.

After coming in the back door of the mayor's office, we found that Mayor Byrne had assembled all of her commissioners and department heads apparently for a special meeting.

The mayor introduced me and explained that I had a special assignment of getting out a tabloid newspaper giving details of all the improvements that were planned for the city for the coming year.

"We want to get this tabloid out within a few weeks so that it can be included as an insert in both the *Tribune* and the *Sun-Times*," she explained. "So give Tom Buck your fullest cooperation in providing him with all the information that will be needed."

That was the first I had heard about the tabloid newspaper, and as we left the meeting, I explained to Jay that it would be almost impossible to get the paper out in several weeks without some help.

"You're free to get help from some of your retired friends at the *Tribune*," Jay said.

Within a month, a *Tribune* retiree, Bryce Engle, and I published a 16-page tabloid newspaper as an insert in the *Tribune* and the *Sun-Times*, and also a Spanish edition for the Chicago Hispanic newspapers.

As a freelance employee, I worked on Jane Byrne's press secretary's staff for the last year and a half of her term and was her press secretary the last six months.

Jane Byrne was one of the best persons I ever worked for. She was very decisive and positive about what she thought should be done. As an employee, one felt that she had full confidence in you and that she was very supportive. On one occasion a City Hall politician began picking at me in an unnecessarily mean manner. Mayor Byrne called him in and told him to lay off, explaining that what I was doing had her full support.

Usually speechwriting is one of the most difficult and time-consuming jobs of a press secretary. However, for Mayor Byrne, speechwriting was not too demanding. She was an excellent speaker; and instead of a script, she needed only what we called "talking points," or memos on subjects she used for extemporaneous speaking.

It was not an easy time for Mayor Byrne. She had made an untold number of enemies as a woman who had defeated the male-dominated Democratic party. There was no doubt that many of the old-timers in the Democratic political organization, including friends and supporters of the Daley family, had little or no use for Mayor Byrne.

The day before the primary in which Jane Byrne defeated Mayor Michael Bilandic, I and other managers at the Chicago Transit Authority attended a "command performance" luncheon of the Democratic organization. As pronounced by virtually every speaker, the theme of that luncheon was, "We can't let that woman take it away from us."

That's exactly what Jane Byrne did, and many of the party stalwarts could not forget it.

For some years I had wondered if I could combine full-time journalism with part-time teaching. Teaching had been a tradition in our family, and I wanted to see if I could do it.

My mother taught school before she was married and again after my father died. A first cousin, Mildred Herd, who grew up in our family, also was an elementary school teacher for many years and during the latter part of her career was a principal in Richmond, Indiana.

My interest in education was probably one of the reasons I became a member of the board of the Evanston Elementary School District No. 65. That was such a turbulent experience that it could be the subject of another book of an entirely different nature.

Because of my desire to teach, I sought the help of a good friend, Ed Rooney, to become a part-time teacher at Loyola University Chicago. Rooney, who had been a reporter for the *Chicago Daily News* for many years, was a full-time professor of journalism at Loyola.

Beginning in 1980, I spent 12 delightful years teaching at Loyola. My wife, Ruth, thinks it was the most rewarding thing I have ever done.

As an adjunct teacher, I taught at both the main Lake Shore campus and the Water Tower campus downtown. Most of my classes were in reporting and writing, but I also taught feature writing and investigative reporting. In the evening classes at the Water Tower Campus, I also had a fairly large number of older students who were taking courses for degrees while working during the daytime.

Students taking the courses I taught earned three hours of credit, and usually there was one lecture class of two-and-a-half hours each week. Instead of using a textbook, I developed my own teaching materials.

In my lectures I used my own experiences as well as those of others I knew to underscore the points I was making. I believe that things are much easier to remember if they are attached to interesting examples and stories.

Even though the lectures were broken up by a 10-minute intermission, it was still a long time to talk. I took pride in the fact that during my 12 years at Loyola I know of only one student who went to sleep in class. As a rationalization, I always believed that he was ill.

Constant practice in writing, in my opinion, is one of the most important parts of journalism instruction. Each week I gave students assignments to write at least five stories based on a hodge-podge of relevant and irrelevant information. I then critiqued their stories in much the same manner as a copy editor handling news stories.

At our first class, I would tell the students they would have to get used to being edited, even though they might feel that their writing was so good that it should not be touched.

"All of us believe that we are Shakespeare," I would remind them. "But even Shakespeare probably had his editor."

Then I would recall an incident from my days as public affairs manager at the CTA.

I received a call from a man who identified himself as a fact-finder for *The New Yorker* magazine. He explained he was checking on some information in a short story that had been written by Saul Bellow, the Nobel Prize winner.

The short story told about a young boy who accompanied his ne'er-do-well uncle on a streetcar trip from Hyde Park on Chicago's South Side to Evanston, immediately north of Chicago.

In the story, the boy and his uncle took a streetcar on 63rd Street west to Western Avenue and then north on Western Avenue to the Chicago-Evanston city limits at

Friends since rooming together at Indiana University in 1935,
J.E. O'Brien (left) and Tom Buck still share reunions, including
this one with Ruth Buck and Jackie O'Brien (right).

Howard Street. They then walked north two or three blocks
on Asbury to visit the uncle's sister, from whom the uncle
hoped to obtain a loan.

The New Yorker fact-finder wanted to know if Bellow
was correct in writing that Western Avenue had the longest
streetcar route in the world, that in Chicago four blocks
made up a mile, and that streetcars at times could have an
odor that was unusual.

I explained that Bellow was not correct in stating that
Western Avenue had the longest streetcar route. I said that
Western Avenue had the longest *straight* streetcar route but
there was another route—a combination of Clark Street
and Wentworth Avenue—which was the longest streetcar
route.

I went on to say that Bellow also was not correct in saying that four blocks in Chicago were equal to one mile. The correct statement, I explained, would be that eight blocks were equal to one mile.

Saul Bellow was correct, I said, in writing that streetcars sometimes had an unusual odor. This occurred when the electric motors became overheated, I explained.

I later read Bellow's story in *The New Yorker* and found that the editors had made all my corrections, including the fact that Western Avenue was the longest *straight* streetcar route.

At the beginning of every semester, I told my classes that if I could correct Saul Bellow, a Nobel Prize winner, I certainly could edit them when they turned in their weekly writing assignments.

In my reporting and writing classes, I explained that three "E"s represented the objectives of newspapers. The three "E"s, I said, stood for the three newspaper purposes of Enlightenment (Information), Education and Entertainment. Good newspaper writing, I said, should be very simple and easy to understand.

I recalled a conversation I once had with Ralph Budd, the innovative railroad executive who in the early 1950s came out of retirement to be chairman of the CTA. As chairman of the Burlington Railroad, Budd had made railroad history in the early 1930s by sponsoring the development of the streamlined passenger trains known as Zephyrs.

In my conversation with Budd, I said that I had seen some of the material he had written for the CTA and was very impressed by it because of its simplicity.

"That must be because of my many years in railroading," said Budd. "In writing rules and operating directives for a railroad, one always had to make sure that the directives could be understood by every employee, regardless of the amount of his or her education."

Clear and simple writing should be the style of newspapers, I told my students, despite the fact that some papers now seem to be emphasizing literary styles which take more time to read and can be confusing.

I believe that newspapers should refrain from using words that send readers to the dictionary. It's impossible for a newspaper reader to look up words in the dictionary while reading a paper on the bus or the elevated-subway train, or at a coffee shop.

I also urged students to write stories that can be read aloud. Reading stories aloud, I explained, not only is a good way to catch errors but also makes for good, smooth writing. Time permitting, students would do well to write a piece, let it sit overnight and then rewrite it the next day.

Many of the best writers in the world, I explained, had achieved success by working their stories over and over. For instance, Hemingway rewrote the last paragraph of *A Farewell to Arms* more than 20 times. As another example, it was said that Tolstoy rewrote much of *War and Peace* five times.

For several years I also taught night classes in public relations at Roosevelt University in downtown Chicago. For a year, I taught a class in news writing at Medill School of Journalism at Northwestern University in Evanston. A good friend, Professor Richard Hainey, asked me to teach the class as a laboratory session for a course he was teaching in reporting and writing.

It was a very interesting experience. The class, consisting of 15 students, met for the lab session for four hours on Tuesday evening. Each student had a computer for writing the stories during the session.

As the teacher, I would pretend to be either holding a press conference or serving as a news source so that the students could question me to obtain the facts for their stories. Besides providing an exercise in writing, this format gave students the experience of asking questions and taking notes.

The students found it so interesting that seldom if ever did anyone take a break during the four hours. As they wrote the stories on their computers, I could look over their shoulders at the screens and make suggestions for changes. At the end of each four-hour session, I had three stories from each of the 15 pupils to critique before the next session.

A school year at Northwestern consists of three academic quarters, and, after my first quarter experience with the lab class, I could guarantee students in subsequent quarters that they would definitely improve their writing.

If I had the energy, I would still like to be teaching. I found that good teaching requires a continuing effort and that one cannot rest on one's laurels.

In addition to putting just one student to sleep in 12 years of teaching at Loyola, I had one other mishap with a student—or, I should say, a prospective student.

A young man who had failed to show up for a first class at the Water Tower Campus called me and asked if he could still join the class.

I suggested that he drop by my public relations office for a briefing before enrolling. My "office" was a very small room I had rented, which was part of a suite used primarily by a telephone answering service. My office was so small that there was room only for myself with most of the space taken by a large desk, two filing cabinets and a typewriter stand supporting my trusty old manual Underwood.

The young man sat on a chair I had placed in my open door.

Besides my small office, he could see a nearby wall to which were strapped more than 30 telephones. There was a telephone for each of the clients of the answering service. It looked very much like a Rube Goldberg arrangement.

"What are those telephones for?" asked the prospective student, pointing to the phones on the wall.

After I had explained the answering service, the young man then pointed at my old Underwood typewriter.

"What's that?" he asked, indicating that he had never seen a manual typewriter before.

I explained that I had not yet learned how to use a computer and that I still used my old Underwood.

"There must be an easier way to do it," said the young man, as he got up from his chair.

"I'll probably let you know about the class," he said as he left.

I never heard from him again.

POSTSCRIPT

One of the most delightful things about a career in journalism is that it does not have to end, regardless of age— that is, if one has the desire, the energy and the capability to carry on.

To do it right, however, requires a great amount of effort. Producing a good story cannot be taken for granted, and can be done only with detailed research and careful writing. It's a way of earning extra money, but the real reward comes from the feeling of satisfaction of having been creative.

Since 1989, I have had the pleasure of reporting, writing and helping to edit a monthly publication, *LifeTimes*, published by Blue Cross and Blue Shield of Illinois for a circulation of 300,000. With Nikki Smith, Ph.D., as editor, *LifeTimes* gives me an opportunity to handle a variety of stories.

I am looking forward to new assignments.

Index